HIGHER, STEEPER, FASTER

HIGHER, STEEPER, FASTER

The Daredevils Who Conquered the Skies

Lawrence Goldstone

LITTLE, BROWN AND COMPANY

NEW YORK BOSTON

Little, Brown and Company
Hachette Book Group
1290 Avenue of the Americas, New York, NY 10104
Visit us at lb-kids.com

First Edition: March 2017

Little, Brown and Company is a division of Hachette Book Group, Inc.
The Little, Brown name and logo are trademarks of Hachette Book Group, Inc.

The publisher is not responsible for websites (or their content) that are not owned by the publisher.

Airplane image on title and chapter pages © jekson_js/Shutterstock.com
Image credits can be found throughout. No credit is included for images in the public domain.

Library of Congress Cataloging-in-Publication Data
Names: Goldstone, Lawrence, 1947– author.
Title: Higher, steeper, faster : the daredevils who conquered the skies / Lawrence Goldstone.
Description: First edition. | New York : Little, Brown and Company, [2017] | Audience: Ages 8 to 12. |
    Includes bibliographical references and index.
Identifiers: LCCN 2016016576| ISBN 9780316350235 (hardcover) | ISBN 9780316350228 (ebook)
Subjects: LCSH: Air pilots—History—Juvenile literature. | Daredevils—History—Juvenile literature. |
    Air pilots—Biography—Juvenile literature. | Daredevils—Biography—Juvenile literature. |
    Flight—History—Juvenile literature. | Aeronautics—History—Juvenile literature.
Classification: LCC TL547 .G64 2017 | DDC 629.13092/2—dc23
LC record available at https://lccn.loc.gov/2016016576

ISBNs: 978-0-316-35023-5 (hardcover), 978-0-316-35022-8 (ebook)

Printed in the United States of America

LSC-C

10 9 8 7 6 5 4 3 2 1

To Nancy and Lee

CONTENTS

Part IV: Pushing to the Edge and Beyond

HIGHER,
STEEPER,
FASTER

Introduction

THE MAN
WHO OWNED THE SKY

March 14, 1915. San Francisco, California

Fifty thousand people sat in the grandstand of the Panama-Pacific International Exposition, facing the bay, and perhaps one hundred thousand more lined the waterfront. The Panama-Pacific was the biggest, most important event ever staged in San Francisco, a world's fair to announce that the city had finally recovered from the terrible 1906 earthquake.

Millions would come to see its attractions: walk-through replicas of Yellowstone National Park and the Grand Canyon, a five-acre working model of the Panama Canal, the actual Liberty Bell, on loan from Philadelphia. The Ford Motor Company had set up an assembly line and for three hours a day would build an automobile every ten minutes. Fairgoers could watch hula dancers, ride a miniature railway or a submarine, or sit in a compartment on a swing arm that propelled those inside to and fro over the grounds. There was even a 435-foot-high Tower of Jewels, decorated with more than one hundred thousand pieces of polished colored glass, called Novagems, imported from Europe and strung on wires. Fifty colored spotlights shone on the tower each night, making it visible in every corner of what was now known as "the Jeweled City." For local children, many of whom lived without plumbing or electricity, the fair was a door to another world.

But on this day, those thousands and thousands of people had not come to see automobiles, submarines, the Liberty Bell, or even a jeweled tower that seemed to stretch all the way to the heavens.

They had come to see a man attempt the impossible. They had come to see Lincoln Beachey fly.

In a hangar, out of sight of the crowd, Beachey checked his airplane. He was a short man, only five feet seven inches, and stocky, with a shock of red hair. Just eleven days before, he had celebrated his twenty-eighth birthday. He was wearing his trademark flying outfit—a pin-striped suit, a two-carat diamond stickpin in his cravat, and a peaked cap that he would turn backward before taking off. In public, Beachey always appeared serious, all business. Few could remember ever seeing him smile.

Beachey pulled at one of the thin cables that braced the wing to the fuselage. He would check every piece of every airplane in which he flew, but never more closely than today. It was taut, with no give. Just right.

And it would have to be just right. This day, Lincoln Beachey was to attempt a feat of flying that no man or woman had tried before, one so dangerous that other flyers had begged him not to try.

But Lincoln Beachey hadn't become the greatest, most celebrated aviator in the world by shrinking from danger. In the United States, he was a better-known figure than President Woodrow Wilson. In a country with a population of almost eighty million people, it had been said that more than twenty million Americans had seen Lincoln Beachey work his magic in the skies above them. For his incredible flying, he made more money in one day than most Americans earned in a year. Reporters called him "the Master Birdman," or "the Man Who Owns the Sky."

He had gained those accolades through a series of daring and harrowing maneuvers. Four years earlier, at the great Chicago International Aviation Meet of 1911, the highest anyone had ever flown was 11,150 feet, and Beachey had been determined to claim the record for himself. But there was only one way to do so. He would need to use all his fuel *on the way up.* That would leave him in the thin, freezing air with no way down but to glide more than two miles in the strong, swirling winds over Lake Michigan, left totally to the mercy of crosscurrents and updrafts. Flying without power—called "dead-sticking"—was one of the most difficult maneuvers any flyer could attempt. Doing so from as low as two hundred feet takes incredible skill. From eleven thousand feet, coming in over water, where the tiniest error meant losing control and plunging to certain death, it was considered impossible. No other person on earth would consider such a stunt.

And the airplane Beachey was to take aloft wasn't even really an airplane at all; at least not the way we would think of one today. It was just a frame, totally open, with wings, a motor, a rudder, and a seat. There was nothing to protect him from the terrible cold and wind at higher altitudes, or to cushion him from jolts worse than the bucking of a bull in a rodeo. Early airplanes had no instruments, not even a fuel gauge to tell flyers when fuel was running out; nothing to tell them where they were, or how high, or if something had gone wrong with the motor. And if something *did* go wrong, there was no way to communicate with the ground. All that protected Beachey and aviators like him from horrible death was their own skill and experience.

For many, that was not enough.

At five thirty PM on August 20, 1911, Beachey got into his airplane. The crowd of 350,000 people fell silent. There was no one else in the air— every eye was focused on him. Beachey took off easily and "ascended steadily, first in circles around the borders of Grant Park and then in wide sweeps that swung him out over the city and then over the lake." With the sky totally clear, Beachey was never out of eyeshot of the ground. Eventually, his airplane seemed no larger than a speck in the sky. But then, after a few moments, the speck began to grow larger. Soon it had

Lincoln Beachey at the controls.

taken shape enough for those on the ground to see that, indeed, his propeller was not moving! He had used all his fuel.

But somehow, although the airplane wobbled and dipped as Beachey descended through the air of the "Windy City," he kept control. "One great circle carried him several hundred yards out over the lake and curved back over Michigan Avenue. His third circle was more nearly around the flying course and his fourth and fifth narrowed as he neared the earth. At the north end of the field he seemed almost to shoot downward." As he neared the ground, the great crowd watching him could hardly breathe— could Beachey actually land the craft safely?

He could and he did! At about seven thirty PM, after more than a two-mile, fifteen-minute glide, Beachey set his airplane down not ten yards from where he had taken off. The tension broke and the spectators erupted in applause. After careful examination and testing, it was determined that Beachey had ascended to 11,642 feet above Lake Michigan. The altitude record was his. It was a feat of flying so incredible that without hundreds of thousands of people there to witness it, pilots even today would refuse to believe it actually happened.

But the Chicago altitude record was merely one of Beachey's remarkable achievements. He had been the first man to fly at Niagara Falls and the first to successfully pull out of a tailspin. He was the first American to fly upside down and to loop the loop. He was the only man to have flown a plane *indoors*, through a huge exhibition building at this very Panama-Pacific fair. He had won innumerable races and set altitude records. He flew the Barrel Roll, the Corkscrew Twist, and every other trick that had ever been attempted.

And one trick that hadn't: a trick that no other flyer could do, although more than a dozen had died trying. He would take his airplane three thousand, even five thousand feet into the sky and then dive—straight down. Sometimes he would turn off his engines; sometimes he would hold his arms out at his sides and control the airplane with his knees. Just when he was so close to the ground that it seemed nothing could prevent a horrible crash, Beachey would pull the airplane out and either gently land or fly off to perform more stunts.

It was a unique trick with a unique name: the Dip of Death.

The Dip of Death had become Beachey's signature maneuver, what all those millions across America had paid to see.

But he had never performed "the Dip" as he would today. For the first time ever, for his hometown crowd, Lincoln Beachey would complete the Dip of Death in a monoplane. One set of wings instead of two.

The monoplane was the future—Beachey knew that. The top wing on a biplane didn't do anything really, except hold the craft together. The cables would work just as well.

Still, he had never flown a monoplane in an exhibition before.

He had designed this airplane himself. He had chosen aluminum, the new miracle metal, for the wings and fuselage, lighter than steel and even stronger. In the thirty years since researchers had discovered how to manufacture it, hundreds, if not thousands, of uses had been found for aluminum. It had even been used to line the dome in the Library of Congress building.

He could have chosen any city in the world—New York, London, Paris—to use his monoplane for the first time, and likely a million people would have turned out, but where better than his hometown to advance aviation's boundaries just that much further?

Lincoln Beachey finished his safety check. The airplane was exactly the way he wanted it. Faintly, he heard the megaphone man begin his

Library of Congress: Chronicling America

Amy Beachey, eighty-one, watching her son fly a biplane at the Panama-Pacific International Exposition.

introduction. Walking up and down in front of the packed grandstand, he trumpeted, "Laaa-dies and gentlemen, don't move from your seats. You are about to witness the premier birdman of them all performing a feat of derring-do that no other man has mastered. Twelve of the greatest aviators in the world have plunged to horrible deaths trying to match him. Today, for the very first time in a monoplane, Lincoln Beachey will perform 'the Dip of Death.'"

That was his cue. Beachey adjusted the diamond stickpin, turned his cap backward, and put on his flying goggles. He climbed into the open cockpit, slipped his arms into the shoulder harness, and signaled his mechanic to crank her over.

As he began to taxi from the maintenance shed to the front of the grandstand, even the roar of the engine could not drown out the cheers of the crowd that grew louder every second.

It was time to make history.

This is the story of the pioneers of flight. Not so much the inventors, as the men and women who *flew*. These were the test pilots before there were test pilots—almost impossibly brave men and women who floated in balloons and with makeshift wings, soared in gliders, and finally piloted powered airplanes. They blazed a trail for every flyer, jet pilot, and even astronaut who came after them. Like every pioneer, they were drawn to riches or fame or simply the same need to explore the unknown that sent primitive sailing ships across the oceans centuries before. And the airplanes that these flyers took into the skies were every bit as primitive as those sailing ships, were every bit as dangerous, and took every bit of bravery just to climb aboard, for every time someone did, death might be waiting.

But because of these remarkable men and women, for whom pushing forward the boundaries of human experience often seemed more important than life itself, the first years of powered flight became one of the most exciting and important eras in human history.

Part I

Birds and Balloons

Chapter 1

THE FIRST BIRDMAN

Even cave dwellers held fantasies of sailing through the air like birds. And for many, many centuries, people thought they could do that by *being* birds, or at least copying them. Ancient Greece had its fable of Icarus, who steered through the sky on wings made of wax and feathers. Then, ignoring his father's warning, Icarus flew too close to the sun. The wax melted, and he fell into the sea and died. Later, wealthy Romans, hoping to discover the secret of bird flight (and smart enough not to try it themselves), strapped wings on their slaves and sent them off tall buildings or cliffs, almost always to their deaths.

The greatest scientists in history tried to decipher the enigma of flight. Leonardo da Vinci sought to diagram a flying machine, as did Isaac Newton. For centuries, inventors tried and failed to keep themselves in the air. With every failure, the dream of flight grew stronger. But the first successes were not with wings but rather giant bags filled with gas. The first came on June 4, 1783, when two brothers, Joseph-Michel and Jacques-Étienne Montgolfier, built, and Jacques-Étienne successfully piloted, a manned balloon over Annonay, France.

Balloons quickly became all the rage. There is no describing the awe men and women felt floating in the air and, for the first time in human history, being able to look down at the trees, rivers, villages, and towns below. But still, balloons weren't really "flying." There was no control. A balloon was either "free," and would be taken wherever the wind wished it, or "captive," attached to the ground by a very long rope. The dream of cruising like a bird remained unfulfilled.

So experiments in controlled flight, winged flight, went on. And continued to fail. Then, in 1891, a German engineer named Otto Lilienthal built a fifty-foot hill outside his home near Berlin, Germany. He braced himself against a set of wooden-framed fabric wings and ran down the incline.

To some, Lilienthal would have seemed ridiculous; just another crazy amateur trying to do what hadn't worked for the Romans. But Otto Lilienthal was no amateur. He had studied flight for thirty years and knew more about "airfoils"—the shape of wings—than any man alive. Using a "whirling arm" that he invented, he had taken tens of thousands of measurements of various-shaped surfaces moving at different angles through the air. He wrote a book on the subject, *Der Vogelflug als Grundlage der Fliegekunst: Ein Beitrag zur Systematik der Flugtechnik* (Birdflight as the basis of aviation: A contribution toward a system of aviation), which would become perhaps the most influential text ever written on flight.

After decades of research, when he thought he had finally solved the problem, Otto Lilienthal built his set of glider wings to the dimensions he had determined from his calculations. He waited for wind conditions to be right, ran down his man-made hill...and soared.

Over the next five years, Lilienthal made more than two thousand flights, gathering knowledge and improving his design. He maneuvered in the air by shifting his weight, usually by kicking his feet. Photographers began to follow his every move, and images of the

Otto Lilienthal's "whirling arm" for testing wing shapes, from an illustration in his book.

first "birdman" were soon making their way around the world.

But to fly, even in a glider only fifty feet off the ground, Lilienthal needed luck as well as skill. On August 9, 1896, his luck ran out. Experimenting with a movable tail, he stalled and then fell, breaking his spine. The next day, Otto Lilienthal died. In his last hours, he uttered one of aviation's most famous sayings: "Sacrifices must be made."

News reports describing Lilienthal's accident spread across the globe, including to Dayton, Ohio, and the headquarters of the Wright Cycle Company, Wilbur and Orville Wright, proprietors. Word of Otto Lilienthal's death, as Wilbur put it, "aroused a passive interest which had existed since my childhood." And so two brothers that no one outside their small community had ever heard of set themselves to furthering the work Otto Lilienthal had begun. They started with what they saw as the natural next step to Otto Lilienthal's wings: gliders.

But the Wright brothers were not alone in attempting to advance Lilienthal's research. Nor did everyone agree that wings should be the basis of flight. In California, one of the world's most famous daredevils—and greatest showmen—was certain that balloons were aviation's future. And he intended to convince everyone else. In doing so, he would not only persuade millions of men, women, and children across America that flight was truly possible but also that it was something that one day, just maybe, they would be able to do themselves.

Chapter 2

PARACHUTES AND GASBAGS

Thomas Scott Baldwin was surely the most unique and entertaining of all aviation's pioneers. Before turning his attention to balloons, he had traveled the world, astounding audiences with his exploits and captivating them with his storytelling. For him, sticking to the truth was never as important as spinning a good yarn. With a dazzling string of accomplishments, he didn't need to tell tall tales—he just seemed to enjoy them. He was born in either Missouri in 1854 or Illinois in 1857, although he later claimed to have begun life in a log cabin in 1861. His parents seemed to have died of natural causes when he was about twelve, although Baldwin later told reporters he had seen them gunned down before his eyes by Confederate renegades during the Civil War.

While still a teenager, Baldwin was hired as a circus tumbler—his specialty was performing tricks on the tops of moving freight trains. He soon moved on to the trapeze and the high wire. "I learned in walking the tightrope that it is not so much a matter of practice or strength as it is in keeping at it until you have the feel of confidence, and when once this comes, a man is equally at home on wire, rope or ground."

Tom Baldwin always had amazing instincts about what people would pay to see. In 1885, he took that skill to San Francisco, a fast-growing city where fortunes could be made. He decided to get the public's attention by walking a tightrope from the balcony of Cliff House to Seal Rocks and back, a round trip of nine hundred feet over pounding surf.

He made headlines, but Tom Baldwin wanted to achieve something

Cliff House and Seal Rocks.

even grander, something no other man could match. And for that, he looked to ballooning. Balloon flights were impressive and always drew crowds, but Baldwin decided to add a new wrinkle. He would rise up in a captive balloon and then parachute out.

Parachutes had been around for almost a century, but they were stiff, rigid, and extremely unreliable. If positioned incorrectly, a parachute would fail to catch the wind and send its unfortunate passenger hurtling helplessly downward at ever-increasing speed until he was crushed on the ground below. If Baldwin was to live to enjoy his riches, he would need to invent a more trustworthy device. He used silk for the canopy, added vents, and then tied ropes between the edge and a large ring underneath. This arrangement allowed his parachute to better right itself in the air. Like most daredevils, Baldwin thoroughly tested his theories before risking his life on them.

"I experimented with sand bags just my own weight and did not venture a jump until I had the 'feel' that it could be safely done. I made most of my jumps in water, and if it had not been that every particle of my body was hard as iron from former training as a gymnast and taking of all kinds of jolts, I would not have lasted through these early experiments."

But designing the parachute was only part of the problem; the other was keeping himself attached to it. Baldwin decided not to build a harness—the scarier the jump, the more money he could ask to risk his life. Instead, he would grasp the wooden ring that held the

Baldwin's Lost Opportunity

Baldwin never bothered to apply for a patent on his parachute and so lost a good deal of money when his design was copied by others.

cords, trusting that a gust of wind would not jerk the ring out of his powerful acrobat's hands. When he was ready, it was time to make the sale.

"I went to Mr. Morton of the Market Street Cable Line and told him I thought I had an exhibition that would be a good feature for the Golden Gate Park, and he asked me what it was, and I told him a parachute jump. I said I would jump for a dollar a foot, and he answered: 'Go ahead and jump a thousand feet!'"

Baldwin's parachute might have been an improvement over earlier models, but, unlike modern parachutes, there was no way to control his direction in the air, so Baldwin risked drifting out over the water or becoming entangled in tree branches. But he did not, and in January 1887, Thomas Baldwin floated gently to the ground below and claimed his $1,000 prize (worth somewhere between $25,000 and $30,000 in 2017 dollars). Afterward, he began to tour the country, venturing higher and higher for greater prize money.

As his reputation grew, plain old "Tom Baldwin" simply would not do. Although his schooling had ended when he ran away from an orphanage at fourteen, he dubbed himself "Professor Baldwin." Eventually he changed that to "Captain Baldwin," which reporters shortened to "Cap't Tom."

In May 1888, in Minneapolis, the "Professor" performed his greatest feat. He allowed the balloon to take him five thousand feet into the air, and then parachuted to the ground for his usual dollar-a-foot fee.

After that, he crossed both oceans, performing in Europe and in Asia in venues as exotic as Thailand, which was then called Siam. His audiences included the cream of society, and even members of royal families. In England, for example, Edward, Prince of Wales, later King Edward VII, was so dazzled by the wonder of a man leaping from a balloon and floating to earth with nothing but his own strength keeping him alive that he reportedly gave Baldwin his own diamond ring after a performance.

As he traveled the globe, Baldwin turned his attention from the parachute to the balloon that carried it. Captive balloons could not go anywhere, and free balloons *might* go anywhere. He decided that the future was in "airships"— balloons that could transport passengers to their desired destinations. That meant mounting a motor on a balloon so that it could sail against the wind, designing a propeller to move it forward, and finding some way to steer. Steerable balloons were called "dirigible."

While he was performing in Germany, Cap't Tom met with Count Zeppelin to learn about the new science of aerodynamics. He also decided that the recently invented internal combustion engine would work best for the power source he sought.

But Cap't Tom wasn't the only person with that idea. In October 1901, Alberto Santos-Dumont, a young Brazilian coffee heir living in Paris, stunned the world—and won 100,000 francs

Count Zeppelin

Ferdinand von Zeppelin was a German army officer who served as an observer with the Union army in the American Civil War. After watching captive balloons, which were used for reconnaissance, he returned home and spent the rest of his life designing airships.

Prize Winnings

In 1901, one dollar was worth five francs, so Santos-Dumont won the equivalent of $20,000. That would be worth $500,000 in 2017.

Engines

The modern version of the internal combustion engine was developed by Nikolaus Otto in 1876. In 1884, Karl Benz mounted a gasoline engine on a three-wheeled vehicle, which is generally thought of as the first automobile.

bicycle pedals to start a small gasoline engine.

But there were many who thought the successful Eiffel Tower circuit was due more to luck and wind currents than brilliant design. (In one of his many other attempts, Santos-Dumont had drifted into the wall of a hotel and was left hanging from the roof after the hydrogen gas in his balloon exploded.) Even Santos-Dumont himself admitted that trying to propel a balloon through the air was "like pushing a candle through a brick wall." In order to gain sufficient

for himself—by successfully navigating a motorized balloon around the Eiffel Tower and returning to his starting point. A small man of barely one hundred pounds, Santos-Dumont wore only the best clothes, dined nightly at the best restaurants, and counted among his close friends Gustave Eiffel, the tower's designer; the jeweler Louis Cartier; and members of many royal families. On his trip around Eiffel's tower, he used

Alberto Santos-Dumont.

thrust—forward power—to give him control in more than a light breeze, Santos-Dumont tried a bigger motor, but it added so much weight that his balloon would not move. Neither he nor anyone else seemed to know quite how to proceed.

Baldwin was stumped as well. Then, in 1904, he "chanced to see a new motorcycle, the motor of which seemed to be exactly what he wanted to propel his new airship." Upon examination, he saw that the machine, called a Hercules, and its lightweight two-cylinder motor had been fashioned by a company called G. H. Curtiss Manufacturing of Hammondsport, N. Y. He sent a telegram and asked to purchase a motor not attached to a frame. The message was received by the firm's owner, a twenty-six-year-old mechanical whiz named Glenn Hammond Curtiss. Curtiss, who had raced motorcycles as well, was puzzled as to why anyone would want the motor without the cycle attached. But an order is an order, so he sent a motor along to California.

Balloon Chemistry

Hydrogen gas had been "discovered" by an English chemist, Henry Cavendish, in 1766, when he treated iron filings with sulfuric acid. The great French chemist Antoine-Laurent de Lavoisier named the substance in 1783, and also confirmed that, with oxygen, hydrogen was one of the two gases that combined to create water. That same year, hydrogen was first used as the substance to lift balloons off the ground.

Curtiss's Land Record

In January 1907, Curtiss would mount an eight-cylinder motor on a bicycle frame and set a land speed record of 136.36 miles per hour at Ormond Beach, Florida.

Curtiss's motor was the last piece of Cap't Tom's puzzle. When he mounted it on his airship, it marked the start of a partnership that would have an immense impact not only on ballooning but on fixed-wing aviation as well.

Chapter 3

INTO THE WIND

In 1904, the worldwide news media of modern times did not exist. Newspapers were, for most people, the only source of information, and most newspapers reported only local or regional events. Many world or national happenings, therefore, passed with no notice by vast segments of the population. And when world news *was* reported, it was often garbled, exaggerated, or simply wrong. So, although there were rumors that two Ohio brothers had conquered the skies, many if not most Americans continued to believe that powered flight was impossible. Among those who did think it was possible to venture aloft, the vast majority thought balloons were the only means to do so. So controlling a balloon, creating a true airship, would be an enormous breakthrough—and make a fortune for the person who did it.

Cap't Tom Baldwin announced that he was that man.

With great fanfare, he took his new airship, which he had named the

California Arrow, to a competition at the Louisiana Purchase Exposition, a world's fair in St. Louis, where an enormous $100,000 prize was offered to anyone who could successfully control an aircraft, of any design. Alberto Santos-Dumont had also brought his latest dirigible to compete for the prize.

The World's Fair

World's fairs began in Europe at the middle of the nineteenth century and brought together industrial and agricultural wonders from around the globe. They were usually staged around a significant event in the host nation, such as the Panama-Pacific International Exposition in San Francisco, at which Beachey flew. The St. Louis fair had opened the year before to commemorate the one hundredth anniversary of the Louisiana Purchase, where, under President Thomas Jefferson, the United States paid France $15 million for 828,000 square miles of territory, almost doubling the nation in size.

In his early years of ballooning, Baldwin had experimented with the giant bags of hydrogen gas. But when he discovered the Curtiss motorcycle, Baldwin was somewhere between forty and fifty years old, and had grown far too heavy to scuttle up and down an inches-wide scaffold to run the motor and keep the ship steady. So, when he arrived in St. Louis, he hired a young newspaperman's son named Roy Knabenshue to pilot the craft.

On October 31, 1904, Knabenshue, whom the newspapers described as a "hero of the air; a good type of American youth," took the *California Arrow* up two thousand feet. Never before had anyone ventured that high in a dirigible. If anything happened so far off the ground, Knabenshue and the balloon would fall like stones and he would have little chance of survival. Just days before, he had crashed in a test run made at much lower altitude, but had gotten away with a few bumps and bruises.

The thousands of spectators who had gathered to see the historic flight were silent as the *California Arrow* took off. Would they be witnessing triumph or tragedy?

"Turning, circling, wheeling this way and that," Knabenshue piloted the airship for thirty-seven minutes, "with the wind and against the wind,"

Library of Congress Prints and Photographs Division

Roy Knabenshue at the Louisiana Purchase Exposition. Note the narrow scaffold underneath, on which the aeronaut would have to scurry back and forth to work the controls while the airship was soaring through the skies.

and then he landed where he had begun. The crowd cheered wildly and the men threw their hats into the air. Baldwin and Knabenshue had done it! They had proved that an airship could be controlled as well as a vehicle on land or sea. "Aeronaut at Fair Accomplishes Greatest Aerial Feat on Record," read the headline in the *St. Louis Republic*.

About the only person who was not pleased was Alberto Santos-Dumont. His balloon had been slashed with a knife by unknown persons as it lay deflated in a warehouse. When local officials suggested that Santos-Dumont had sabotaged the balloon himself because he knew it could not match Baldwin's, the tiny Frenchman, his honor questioned, furiously packed up and left for home.

Baldwin and Knabenshue returned to San Francisco as two of the most famous men in America. So many people wanted to see Cap't Tom's new marvel that he decided one airship was not enough. He would build another and another. All he needed was to find young men—and sometimes young women—who were brave and able enough to pilot them.

Then, one day, while Baldwin was sitting behind his desk, a short, red-haired teenager named Lincoln Beachey walked into his office.

Chapter 4

THE BOY AERONAUT

Beachey had been on his own since he was twelve, when he left school to work. He and his older brother, Hillery, had been raised in poverty. Their father, William, had been blinded fighting for the Union in the Civil War and was unable to work, but had been granted only a meager pension. Their mother, Amy, tried to keep food on the table hiring herself out as a washerwoman. Both brothers ran errands and did odd jobs from the time they were five or six. But Beachey wanted more than the pittance such menial work brought in. A lot more. And he knew precisely how to get it.

Racing.

Bicycle racing was America's most popular sport. Crowds as large as ten thousand people paid to see racers who earned five times what baseball players made, and even more than heavyweight boxing king Bob Fitzsimmons. Champion bicycle racers such as Frank Kramer and Major

Taylor were national heroes. To reach the top, it took skill and nerve, two things Lincoln Beachey was certain he had a lot of.

Of course, he'd first have to earn enough money to buy a bicycle. But the wondrous machines were everywhere. As Beachey was growing up, the bicycle had been perhaps the most popular item ever sold in the United States. Now, at the dawn of the twentieth century, as many as ten million two-wheelers had been sold in the twenty years since the introduction of the "safety bicycle"—one with equal-size front and back wheels. (Before that, the "high wheeler," with its huge front wheel and tiny back one, demanded too much skill just to get on to be popular with ordinary folks.) Small manufacturers had sprung up across the nation, including in Dayton, Ohio, where two brothers named Wright had left the printing business to join in the fad.

Beachey, to no one's surprise (least of all his), immediately established himself as a fearless and daring bicycle racer. And he would never quit, no matter how difficult the course or fierce the competition. A boy, however, even a talented and determined one, was simply not strong or experienced enough to race against men. He entered a two-mile speed trial at fifteen but, despite pedaling furiously and taking turns recklessly, he failed to win a prize. He realized then that for him, the big money was elsewhere. There was another, newer sort of racing, in which his age and inexperience would not work against him. So he turned to motorcycles.

Motorcycles were less than a decade old, little more than powerful engines mounted on bicycle frames. But their speed and sleek design had captured the public's imagination. Races were grand spectacles, with fast-moving two-wheelers taking turns at severe angles, kicking up dirt and stones, or speeding neck and neck down long straightaways. There were crashes in almost every race, some of them fatal. But the greater the danger, the more the public crowded in to see the events.

Even at sixteen, Beachey became one of the most daring and relentless riders in San Francisco. He was so determined to win that after finishing first in one five-mile race, he was disqualified "on the ground of professionalism." That meant he had gone around the track with such fury that he was judged a danger to himself and others. But Beachey always rode under control—it just didn't always look that way.

Soon, even the speed of motorcycles was not enough for a young man who craved the excitement of doing things that no one had ever done before. When Beachey heard of a man named Baldwin in San Francisco who needed someone for a job even more stirring and dangerous than motorcycle racing, he rushed off to meet him. Lincoln Beachey was about to come face-to-face with a man whose fearlessness, charisma, ambition, and thirst for the unknown were every bit the match for his own.

The first time they met, in Baldwin's office, Beachey looked Baldwin straight in the eye and told him he had found his man. Cockiness would have put off some, but Cap't Tom admired self-confidence. The youngster had the perfect body type for the job—he could be quicker and surer along the undercarriage than even the lanky Roy Knabenshue. Acting purely on instinct, Baldwin hired Beachey on the spot.

It turned out to be a brilliant move. Within months, Beachey had shown so much skill piloting Baldwin's airship that he had become more famous than Knabenshue. Newspapers across the nation lauded the skill and daring of the youngster they called the "Boy Aeronaut." The amazing control exhibited by the "blue-eyed lad of seventeen who makes daring

Library of Congress: Chronicling America

The Boy Aeronaut, in a photograph that appeared in newspapers across the nation.

flights in the big Baldwin airship" was such that he was said to make the balloon "do practically everything but turn somersaults."

In September 1905, at an exposition in Portland, Oregon, he completed what reporters called "perhaps the most remarkable flight ever made in an airship." As reported in the *Los Angeles Herald*, "Beachey navigated the huge vessel with wonderful dexterity and precision, at all times having it under perfect control. He made one stop on top of the Chamber of Commerce building, where he delivered a letter. Beachey once more ascended and headed his airship toward the office of the *Oregon Journal*, where he dropped another letter. From the *Journal*, the airship swiftly made its way to the Oregonian Building, where another letter addressed to the *Evening Telegram* was dropped on the roof. From the Oregonian Building, Beachey headed westward toward St. Vincent Hospital, maneuvering high in the air for a few minutes. Beachey then headed the airship for the exposition grounds, where he landed safely."

Afterward, Beachey was asked what it felt like to fly.

"There's really nothing to it. It's just the same as being on the ground so far as nervousness is concerned. I stand on this two-inch beam along the under side of the framework, walk along it when I want to reach some

Library of Congress Prints and Photographs Division

The *California Arrow*.

other part of the ship, and think nothing whatever about being 2,000 feet up in the air; all my thoughts are centered on how to make the ship operate as we expect it to do. It's just as safe up there as it is down here if you don't get scared, and scared people have no business in an airship."

Of course, there was a lot to it. Scurrying up and down a two-inch beam under a balloon that is moving up and down and side to side in the wind would be terrifying to almost anyone. But Lincoln Beachey, as he was to prove throughout his life, was one of those rare people who were genuinely without fear.

The Boy Aeronaut's reputation wasn't hurt by a series of near disasters. In September 1906, while he was "several hundred feet off the ground," the gasoline tank for the motor sprung a leak and caught fire, threatening to ignite the remaining gasoline and the hydrogen in the balloon. Hydrogen burns quickly, so it would have meant a horrible death for Beachey. After trying without success to smother the fire, he leaned over the flimsy rail and opened the relief valve, allowing the remaining gasoline in the tank to run out. With only what "little vapor remained in the engine," Beachey then guided the ship to the ground, where the ground crew tied it up. When he stepped out, both of his hands were burned.

The following year, a broken propeller landed him in the treacherous currents near Hell Gate in New York, where he made his way to a buoy until a passing boat could rescue him.

Beachey's fame was cemented on June 14, 1906, just eleven days after he had narrowly escaped death in Cleveland when a propeller cut the gasbag and sent him plummeting one thousand feet to the ground. On the date that a decade later would become Flag Day, he flew his airship to and then around the most famous building in the United States, the Capitol in Washington, DC.

Congress was in session when Beachey approached the almost three-hundred-foot-high dome that tops the chambers of the United States Senate and House of Representatives. But it did not remain in session for long. Congressmen left their desks to run outside and watch the amazing demonstration "in joyous, neck craning contemplation."

Before he was done, Beachey had flown over most of the city. "Soaring like a bird hundreds of feet above the earth," reported the *Washington Times* on page 1, "dodging tall smokestacks and other obstacles as easily as if he were in an automobile turning corners on a smooth asphalt pavement, Lincoln Beachey, the boy aeronaut, guided an airship grace-fully in a circle from the base to the top of Washington Monument, and then glided over to the White House."

"I alighted in the square on the east front of the Capitol," Beachey said later, "and when I stepped out of the machine I found [Speaker of the House] Uncle Joe Cannon had declared a recess to look at the bal-loon, and I answered questions for an hour before they would let me fly back to Luna Park. I also called on President Roosevelt but he was out in Georgetown so I missed him." Beachey had a chat with Mrs. Roosevelt and a visiting congressman, then returned to the Capitol, where he was treated to lunch by some senators and representatives.

When Beachey soared off, he left Washington in an uproar. Thou-sands had left work to gawk. Later, city residents took to pinning a paper to their lapels that read, "Yes, I saw it."

Among those who saw it were senior officers of the United States Army. Soon afterward, Thomas Baldwin received a contract to build airships for the Signal Corps, not to carry weapons, but to fly reconnaissance missions over enemy lines.

With Lincoln Beachey's help, Thomas Baldwin had convinced many that the future of air travel was dirigible balloons. But an old adversary was about to change everyone's mind.

Library of Congress: Chronicling America

Beachey over Washington, DC.

Part II

Wings

Chapter 5

THE BIRD OF PREY

In August 1906, less than three months after the Boy Aeronaut had amazed Washington, DC, with his air artistry, Alberto Santos-Dumont amazed Paris with his. Certain he had been tricked out of his rightful $100,000 by the promoters of the St. Louis fair, Santos-Dumont had returned home to France in a foul mood. (Baldwin did not receive one penny of prize money, either. The fair's organizers had run through their entire bankroll and used the prize money to keep the fair going.) But rather than sulk, he chose instead to move forward, to take flight beyond the realm of bulky, slow-moving airships to the sleek new world of fixed-wing flight, airplanes.

There had been many successful experiments with gliders in both Europe and America, but adding the weight of a motor and getting the airplane off the ground had everyone baffled. Even if the contraption succeeded in becoming airborne, there was the problem of how to control it. Whoever solved those problems was guaranteed a place in the history books.

As Santos-Dumont set to work, he was aware that those two Ohio brothers, the Wrights, claimed to have flown a fixed-wing aircraft as early as 1903. They called it the Wright Flyer. They had been trying to sell their machines in France, Germany, Great Britain, and the United States. But no one had seen the Wright Flyer fly! The Wright brothers had refused to demonstrate their invention—or even let anyone see it. The Wrights were convinced that they could sell airplanes on their word and a few photographs only. They were wrong, and so few people believed these Americans had actually solved what was known as "the flying problem." In fact, in France, they became known as *bluffeurs*—fakers—for trying to sell a product that did not exist.

Santos-Dumont employed a design unlike that of any of the other experimenters. His wings were a series of box kites mounted at the back of the craft. They were attached to a long body that ended with another box kite at the nose. The machine was held together by piano wire, wrapped around long pieces of pine that ran the length of the craft. Like Baldwin, who had used a motorcycle engine for his airship, Santos-Dumont removed a motor from an automobile and attached it to the rear of the craft, between the wings, just behind where the pilot would stand. This was the

The Fifteenth Creation

Santos-Dumont had numbered his creations from his first balloon to his fourteenth airship. For his first fixed-wing creation, for reasons he never said, he did not use 15, but rather *14bis*—"fourteen extra," or "fourteen encore."

Library of Congress Prints and Photographs Division

Alberto Santos-Dumont in *14bis*.

only aircraft in history in which the pilot was required to stand from take-off to landing.

For the first tests of his invention, Santos-Dumont employed a donkey to pull the odd-looking machine, which he had suspended in the air with a rope and pulley. He then hung *14bis* from a balloon. The tests went well. Despite its appearance, it seemed that *14bis* could actually fly!

And on August 23, 1906, it did...sort of.

On his first attempt, Santos-Dumont, dressed in a perfectly tailored white linen suit, fired up his engine and drove his machine across an entire field, but his motor was not powerful enough to lift *14bis* off the ground. After some tinkering, the motor generated a bit more power and Santos-Dumont got the wheels in the air for some short but significant hops.

But hopping was more than anyone else had done, and Alberto Santos-Dumont made headlines around the world. The tiny aviator told reporters, "I have accomplished more than I dared hope." The news-papermen were not satisfied calling this miraculous craft just *14bis*, so they settled on "Bird of Prey," which was a bit strange for a contraption that had risen less than ten feet off the ground.

Santos-Dumont improved his machine and made more flights in September, October, and November, the last of which kept him airborne for more than seven hundred feet. Around the world, Alberto Santos-Dumont was celebrated as the first man to successfully fly an airplane. As a further reward, he was given a 50,000-franc ($10,000) prize for his achievement.

Yet outside France, perhaps because the *Bird of Prey* had hardly risen off the ground, or had traveled for such a short distance, praise for the accomplishment was oddly muted. After all, powered flight should have been a milestone in human history. American newspapers especially did not at all greet the achievement with banner headlines. In the *New York Times*, for example, the prizewinning flight merited only one small paragraph, and the flights were described as "experiments." Many news-papers ignored the flights entirely. Santos-Dumont's entry in a balloon race across the English Channel—which he lost to an American—got more notice than *14bis*.

Among those who were singularly unimpressed with the Brazilian's exhibitions were Wilbur and Orville Wright. They thought Santos-Dumont's design was flawed, even silly, incapable of achieving anything beyond short, bouncing runs across cleared land. A real airplane would do much, much more.

And they intended to prove it.

Chapter 6

TAKEOFF!

The French press had been badly mistaken. The Wright brothers were not *bluffeurs*. As all of France would soon find out, they had done everything that they had claimed and created an airplane that was everything *14bis* was not.

Wilbur Wright began working on the "flying problem" in 1896, by studying in the Dayton Library. When he thought he had learned enough to take a real stab at getting a glider in the air, he wrote to the Smithsonian Institution in Washington, DC, the leading scientific organization in America. He asked for anything they could send him on aeronautics.

Few people would have expected Wilbur Wright to solve the riddle of flight. He had never studied engineering nor even finished high school. Except for bicycles, he had no experience with any form of mechanical transportation.

But Wilbur Wright was a genius, one of the greatest instinctive scientists America has ever produced. And he possessed an unbreakable will. Once Wilbur began a task, nothing could keep him from working on it until he had succeeded.

By the time he wrote his letter, he was already forming the idea that would unlock the secret to controlled flight. After months and months of watching birds—buzzards, because of their immense wingspan, were his favorites—he noticed two things. The first was that wind was necessary. "No bird soars in a calm," he said. The other was that birds moved their wing tips in an unusual way when they turned. In order to turn or keep steady, the tip of one wing would rise while the tip of the other would drop.

When he was not trying to figure out how to fly, Wilbur worked with Orville at the Wright Cycle Company. From riding bicycles, Wilbur came to understand that control was the crucial element of flight. Getting an aircraft off the ground would not be a huge problem. The many successful glider experiments by aviation pioneers around the world had proved that. Powering it once it was in the air would also not be difficult. A small motor would work nicely and not add too much weight. The dilemma was what to do once the machine was airborne.

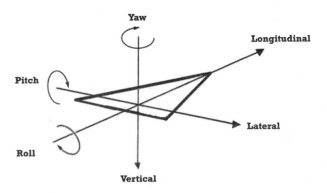

The three axes of motion.

To control an airplane, especially to turn one, three axes of motion must be accounted for: side to side (yaw), laterally (roll), and front to back (pitch).

From there Wilbur Wright made his most brilliant and inventive leap. He decided that others who were trying to fly were making a huge error—to control their craft, they were trying to make it as stable as possible, preventing roll. Once roll began, it would continue to get worse until the airplane entered a deadly spin that would send the machine crashing to earth. To prevent roll, they set their wings moving up from the center—like *14bis*—in what is called a "dihedral."

While preventing the craft from falling into a deadly spin, it also made an airplane very difficult to turn or even to fly in a straight line in swirling winds.

Wilbur had a different idea. Instead of avoiding roll, he would use it,

Dihedral Wings

Dihedral wings are self-correcting; that is, if a roll begins—because of wind currents, perhaps—the wing that moves higher exerts less "lift," so it tends to return to where it started. Only when the airplane is level do both wings exert the same lift.

Wings in a dihedral.

just like a bicyclist. If a bicyclist did not slightly bank in a turn, employ "roll," he or she would likely end up in the bushes or sprawled in the road. Wilbur would, therefore, bank his airplane in a turn.

To allow his airplane to roll, he would set the wings in an "anhedral," whereby the wings slope down from the center.

Wings in an anhedral.

From there, all Wilbur needed to do was to find a way to control the airplane when it rolled. That would stop a spin and allow the airplane to bank on a turn, just as with a bicycle. For that, he used what he had observed in birds. "If the rear edge of the right wing tip is twisted upward and the left downward, the bird instantly begins to turn." He decided to apply that principle to his airplane.

In July 1899, Wilbur built a kite to test his theory. Its wings were

Visiting the Flyer

The original Wright Flyer is on exhibit at the Air and Space Museum in Washington, DC, part of the Smithsonian Institution, to which Wilbur wrote his famous letter in 1896. The anhedral wing arrangement is plainly visible.

about six feet across, set in an anhedral. He added four strings that he could pull like a puppeteer to make one end of the kite move up while the other moved down. He called this "wing-warping." He flew the kite for some local schoolboys while Orville was on a camping trip and found that, yes, he really could control the kite by twisting the sets of wings in opposite directions. From there, the next step was to build one large enough to carry a man.

But to design his kite to carry so much weight, Wilbur first had to teach himself engineering. Otherwise he would be unable to make any sense of the equations and formulas he was encountering in books. He wrote away for even more material and then spent as many hours learning

Library of Congress Prints and Photographs Division

Wilbur landing after testing a glider at Kitty Hawk in 1900.

how to use what he found as he had studying birds. By summer 1900, he was ready. From the National Weather Service, he learned that the remote Atlantic islands off the coast of North Carolina had constant light winds and sandy beaches, exactly what was needed to test the new glider and make certain he wasn't hurt in crashes. But his destination, Kitty Hawk, was a desolate outpost, with few people, fewer houses, no grocery stores or any other of the comforts that he had taken for granted in Dayton. Before he could perfect his kite, he would have to build a camp.

He engaged his brother, Orville, who until then had been involved only in the bicycle business, and in September 1900, they pitched their tent for the first time in Kitty Hawk. That season lasted only three weeks and proved a terrible disappointment. Despite all of Wilbur's calculations, and the success with his simple kite, they could not get the bigger model to work as they had expected.

But the Wrights would not be discouraged and they returned to Kitty Hawk for three more years. They endured bad weather, isolation, terrible food, swarms of mosquitoes, crashes, and many other failures. They made countless adjustments to the shape of the wings, the rudder, and their wing-warping controls. Lying in the center of the airplane reduced wind resistance so that the small motor they would install could more easily power them off the ground. Their airplane had no wheels, so they installed a track in the sand and assigned whichever brother that was not flying to run alongside during takeoff to keep the wings from tipping and striking the sand.

On December 14, 1903, Wilbur Wright attempted to become the first man ever to achieve powered, controlled flight in a fixed-wing airplane. It would be a moment unique in human history. Everyone, everywhere, for centuries to come would remember the Wright brothers. Just after

Wilbur left the ground, however, the craft went nose-first into the sand. A disappointment, but only a brief setback. Wilbur was not hurt, and the brothers were certain their design was sound. The airplane was repaired and minor adjustments made.

Three days later, it was Orville's turn. And this time, everything worked! On December 17, 1903, the Wright Flyer made four successful flights and a problem that had confounded humanity for thousands of years had been solved.

It would be some time, however, before the world knew it.

Library of Congress Prints and Photographs Division

The first flight. One of the most famous photographs in the world.

Chapter 7

SILENT SUCCESS

The Wright brothers had not spent all those years trying to fly for the sake of achievement alone. They intended to make airplanes a business. So before they demonstrated their invention for *anyone*, they hired a lawyer and applied for a patent. A patent is a license granted by the United States Patent Office that protects inventors. It says no one can use a product without the inventor's permission, and that a patent holder can collect money in return for giving that permission. To get a patent, an inventor has to prove that he or she did not copy anyone and actually created something new.

But patents take a long time, usually years. The patent examiners often send back an application with questions, and these must be answered before the application can be approved. In fact, the Wright brothers' lawyer told them not even to include a motor on their design, that it might hold them up even longer. So their application was actually for a glider that used their wing-warping method.

While their application was being considered, Wilbur and Orville were afraid that if others saw the Wright Flyer, someone would steal their ideas and get the patent before they did. So they privately tested and improved their airplane, getting it in shape so that it could be sold. That was why when Tom Baldwin launched his dirigible at the St. Louis fair, no one knew that fixed-wing flight had already been achieved.

By autumn 1905, the Wrights had made enormous strides forward from the machine they had flown at Kitty Hawk. It could now fly for miles and miles, get hundreds of feet off the ground, carve elegant turns,

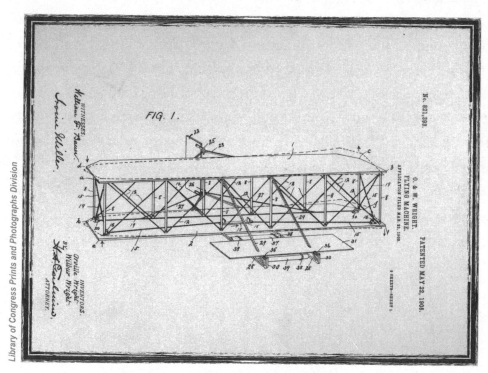

A sketch for the Wright patent. Note the absence of a motor.

and turn figure eights in the air. They installed a seat so that the operator would no longer have to lie prone, and a series of levers to make it easier to control the aircraft in the sky.

They wanted to offer it for sale, but their patent application had still not been approved. Wilbur and Orville decided to try to sell airplanes without actually showing them to anyone. They described what their airplane could do, took photographs, and contacted the United States Army. They also tried to interest the governments of France, Great Britain, and Germany. They offered to fly their airplane once someone signed a contract to buy Wright Flyers, but no one would.

On May 22, 1906, their patent was finally granted. But even then, for reasons they never stated, the Wrights continued to refuse to fly their airplane in public without a signed contract. When it became clear that no one would pay for something without first seeing it work, Wilbur and Orville finally agreed to demonstrate the Flyer for a reporter for *Scientific American*. The reporter was dazzled. He had never seen nor even imagined what the improved Wright Flyer could do in the air. But the reporter added that never in history had anyone done something so important without announcing it.

But in August 1906, when Alberto Santos-Dumont flew *14bis* in Paris, keeping the Wright Flyer secret ceased to be an option.

Chapter 8

TRIUMPH...

Soon after Santos-Dumont made headlines, Wilbur and Orville packed a Flyer into crates and shipped it to France. They intended to fly there in 1907, but the airplane was damaged by customs agents and the exhibition could not take place until the following year. The Wrights also agreed to demonstrate the Flyer for the United States Army at Fort Myer near Washington, DC. Those tests would be in September 1908. If the airplane performed as promised, the army would purchase a number of them for use on scouting missions.

On August 8, 1908, Wilbur made the first public flight of a Wright Flyer at Hunaudières racetrack near Le Mans, 135 miles from Paris. It lasted only two minutes, but by the time he landed, aviation was changed forever. The French, who thought they were first in flying, were left gasping. Alberto Santos-Dumont's contraption was a toy compared to this marvel they watched soar above them.

Over the next two weeks, Wilbur made about ten more flights, none of them more than eight minutes. He flew easily, turning in deep banks, carving circles and even figure eights in the sky, all with control of the aircraft far beyond anything anyone had seen or even imagined before. In the face of such brilliant flying, there was no more talk of *bluffeurs*. The French pretended that they had believed Wilbur all along. "Frenchmen seemed to vie with each other in giving the praise and credit so long over-due," one reporter wrote, "and all hasten to say 'never had any doubts.'"

As he grew more confident in the Flyer's abilities, Wilbur began to make longer flights. He became a celebrity in a country where he had been laughed at only two months before. On September 6, after a flight

Library of Congress Prints and Photographs Division

Wilbur in France. Tens of thousands came to watch him fly.

of almost twenty minutes, Wilbur wrote Orville that "the newspapers continue to be exceedingly friendly and the public interest and enthusiasm continues to increase." He was invited to dinner with the best of French society, the sort of people with whom Alberto Santos-Dumont regularly dined, although the Brazilian did not join them. But Wilbur had problems in the strange country as well. His French was poor, so he could not find anyone to help work on the Flyer who could understand what he was saying. And he needed a mechanic, because the Flyer's motor kept breaking down.

But all difficulties were overcome. On September 16, Wilbur made headlines around the world by keeping the Flyer in the air for nearly forty minutes, covering twenty-nine miles at an average speed of forty-six miles per hour. All three marks were official records, meaning that the measurements were taken by judges appointed by government or private aeronautical organizations.

Wilbur made sure to keep up on the news from home, where Orville was practicing his test flights for the army. "The newspapers for several days have been full of the stories of your dandy flights," he wrote to Orville on September 13.

Orville deserved the praise. On September 9, he had amazed onlookers by flying, unofficially, for fifty-seven minutes over the Fort Myer parade ground, traveling an estimated forty miles, landing only to make a minor repair to his motor. He then returned to the air, this time staying aloft for sixty-two minutes and reaching speeds of fifty miles per hour. A third flight lasted only six minutes, but he made it with a passenger sitting next to him. During the practice runs at Fort Myer, Orville flew higher, farther, and faster than anyone had before. His banked turns caused the same gasps in the United States as had Wilbur's in France.

Library of Congress Prints and Photographs Division

Orville at Fort Myer.

"He drove his ship down the field far past the aerodrome and into the broken country beyond. Over the roofs of the post buildings he sailed, and he looked down on the graves in Arlington through the tree tops ninety feet beneath," gushed a reporter.

But Orville was about to make a flight that would not be at all dandy, and afterward neither he nor aviation would ever be the same.

Arlington

Arlington National Cemetery is a military cemetery where men and women who have fought in America's wars are buried. The grounds had been the site of Confederate general Robert E. Lee's plantation, which was taken over by the United States government and established for its present use after the Civil War.

Chapter 9

...AND TRAGEDY

By September 17, 1908, all that remained for Orville at Fort Myer was the official test. Few had any doubts that the Flyer would pass easily.

Glenn Curtiss and Tom Baldwin were at Fort Myer as well, for dirigible trials. Baldwin's entry was twice the size of the *California Arrow* and was powered by a twenty-five-horsepower Curtiss motor. The propeller had been designed by the army's aviation expert, twenty-six-year-old Lieutenant Thomas Selfridge. While Orville's flights had grabbed the headlines, Baldwin's high-flying airship also impressed army officers. Because it could stay in the air for hours, they thought it might be even more effective for scouting and communication than the Wrights' invention.

Even so, the main attraction was Orville Wright. He had flown brilliantly, but he was piloting an airplane with a new system of lever controls that Wilbur had designed, and they had given him some early trouble. Glenn Curtiss wrote, "The first flight was rather short as Mr. Wright said the levers seemed awkward for him. He made a wrong move and headed into a dive for the tent, which necessitated immediate landing."

As the official trial neared, an officer had to be assigned to ride with Orville as a passenger. Thomas Selfridge got the job. Just after five PM, before two thousand spectators, both men took their places in the Flyer. Orville sat at the controls with Selfridge next to him. The young lieutenant was barely able to contain his excitement. A reporter for the *New York Times* said that Selfridge "looked as eager as a schoolboy for the test to begin."

Library of Congress Prints and Photographs Division

Orville Wright and Thomas Selfridge waiting to begin their flight while a mechanic prepares to spin the propeller.

Orville took off and made three circuits of the field more than one hundred feet off the ground. He flew easily and made beautifully banked turns. People on the ground could see a broad smile on Thomas Selfridge's face.

Then something went wrong.

W. S. Clime, an army photographer, saw what happened. "There was a crack like a pistol shot coming from above. I saw a piece of a propeller blade twirling off.... For a brief period [the aeroplane] kept on its course, then swerved to the left and...backwards...and fell half the distance to the ground. Then it suddenly righted itself for an instant...only to pitch forward and strike on the front, raising an immense cloud of dust that momentarily hid it from view."

There was a rush to the wreckage. Both men were terribly hurt, but Selfridge's injuries were far more serious. The fuel tank and motor had broken loose in the crash and pinned him underneath. He was unconscious and seemed to be choking. With soldiers on horseback on the scene to keep spectators away, both men were removed from the wreckage and rushed to Fort Myer hospital. Although Orville had broken his leg and four ribs, and dislocated his hip, doctors knew he would recover. Selfridge had two fractures of the skull as well as internal injuries. He was wheeled into the operating room as soon as he arrived at the hospital but never regained consciousness. Just before nine PM, Thomas Selfridge, a man destined for greatness, exceptionally bright and universally respected, died.

Powered flight had its first fatality.

The accident was very carefully investigated, and all agreed that Orville bore no blame. He later said that he heard or felt two thumps and then a louder one that shook the airplane. He turned his engines

Library of Congress Prints and Photographs Division

Doctors attending Thomas Selfridge.

off and he thought he had control, but then the nose of the craft suddenly turned upward and the Flyer began to drop, tail first. He pulled the rudder lever but it didn't work. The airplane turned nose down and pitched into the ground below. Orville said that he was regaining control in the seconds before the crash and if he'd had another twenty-five feet of altitude, he might have righted it. With a broken propeller, though, he probably would not have.

The brothers both agreed that Wilbur should remain in Europe, trying to sell airplanes. Orville Wright was in the hospital for six weeks, his sister Katharine by his side. When he was finally discharged, he walked with two canes, then soon after only one. Within weeks, that cane was abandoned as well. Although he never complained, Orville was in pain from the injuries from that crash for the rest of his life.

Chapter 10

CROSSING THE CHANNEL

Although the Wright brothers had now received the acclaim of the entire world for their invention, their delay in publicizing it was about to cause them problems they had not foreseen. Although Wilbur said that it would be many years before other designers began to build workable airplanes, he was mistaken. By the time he flew in France, other men had already begun to do it.

And that meant competition.

In October 1908, the owner of the English newspaper *Daily Mail* offered £1,000 ($5,000 then, $125,000 in 2017) to the first man to fly between England and France across the English Channel. Crossing the Channel back then was like flying to the moon would be in 1969. The person who did it would be hailed as the greatest flyer in the world.

Everyone expected Wilbur Wright to try for the prize, but Wilbur declined. Orville's crash at Fort Myer was still fresh in his mind, and the winds in the Channel were strong and unpredictable. Instead, on the last day of 1908, Wilbur flew for another prize, the Michelin Cup, which was also $5,000. He made a remarkable two-hour-and-nine-minute flight in intense cold at Le Mans, about 135 miles west of Paris. Officially, Wilbur traveled seventy-three miles around a course set in a triangle, but taking his very wide turns into account, he might have gone ninety. That was farther than anyone had flown before.

The Channel flight was only twenty-three miles, but Wilbur continued to refuse to attempt it. Perhaps he felt that the Wright Flyer was the only aircraft capable of completing the journey, and he could afford to wait. If that was the case, he waited too long. By summer 1909, three French aviators announced that they would try for the prize.

It would be aviation's first great quest, and the winner would be anointed as its next great hero.

The first of the entrants was Hubert Latham, who also raced motorboats, was a big-game hunter, and had already floated across the Channel in a balloon at night. Latham was tall and handsome, dressed perfectly, and spoke French, German, and English. Latham would fly the Antoinette IV, a monoplane that had the look of a giant insect. Latham's airplane was designed differently from the Wrights'. The propeller was in the front—such aircraft were called "tractors"—instead of in the back—"pushers."

The Antoinette

The designer was Léon Levavasseur, who would also invent the V-8 engine and fuel injection, both later widely used in automobiles. Levavasseur's Antoinette models were named for his daughter.

Library of Congress Prints and Photographs Division

Hubert Latham in his Antoinette IV.

The second entrant was a French-Russian aristocrat, Charles Alexandre Maurice Joseph Marie Jules Stanislas Jacques, Count de Lambert, who could trace his family lineage back to 1287. Count de Lambert had been the first person personally taught to fly by Wilbur Wright. He said afterward that "the handling of the aeroplane was simplicity itself, and he was confident he would become proficient in a very short time." The count had purchased two Wright Flyers, which he brought to the French coast.

The third man was Louis Blériot. After making a good deal of money by inventing headlamps for automobiles, Blériot had begun to experiment with flying machines in 1903, even before the Wright brothers flew at Kitty Hawk. For years, he had been unable to get anything off the ground. Finally, in 1907, he built a monoplane, the Blériot VII. (Like Santos-Dumont, Blériot numbered his experiments.) The VII was a clumsy, poor-handling craft, but it could get into the air for short distances. After that, however, Blériot made real progress. He was certain his latest, the Blériot XI, was the airplane that would cross the Channel.

Physically, Blériot was Latham's opposite. He was short, heavy, and not especially handsome. He wore a thick mustache, which gave him something of a comical appearance, like a character in the popular French theater the Comédie-Française.

Most people thought Latham would be the victor. The Antoinette seemed the most advanced aircraft, even more so than the Wright Flyer. Early in the morning of July 19, Latham took off from Calais, on the French coast. On both sides of the Channel, huge crowds cheered.

Louis Blériot.

Library of Congress Prints and Photographs Division

Latham's Antoinette.

Motorboats and yachts sailed on the rough water. Everyone wanted to catch a glimpse of Latham flying into history—or to be ready for a rescue if history was not to be made that day. Indeed, Latham got only about a third of the way across. His engine stalled and he and the Antoinette were dumped into the waves. But the crippled airplane did not sink. When a rescue ship arrived, Latham was sitting calmly on his airplane, smoking a cigarette from an ivory cigarette holder, the waters washing over him. As soon as he stepped out on dry land, he ordered another airplane and vowed to make a second try.

Count de Lambert never even got over the water. Both of his Wright Flyers crashed on the shore during practice runs—flying, it turned out, was not quite as simple as the count had thought.

Latham's new airplane was soon delivered, and he and Blériot waited for the howling Channel winds to die down. Blériot was in terrible pain. He had suffered third-degree burns on his left foot in an accident while testing out the Blériot XI. He needed crutches to walk and would strap them to his airplane so that he might make his way about when he reached England—if he reached England.

Finally, just after midnight on July 25, the wind dropped. This was the chance the remaining two flyers had been waiting for. Blériot and his wife were awakened at two in the morning. He ate breakfast, tested the aircraft, and waited for both sunrise and Latham. It would be a race to reach England. But Latham never appeared. His assistant had forgotten to wake him. At four thirty AM, Blériot took off—alone.

Blériot over Calais.

Ten minutes later, Louis Blériot disappeared into the mist that hung over the water. His wife was on the ship that was supposed to rescue him if the plane went down, but no one could see or hear a thing. Madame Blériot was terrified. Her husband was wearing a life belt made out of cork, but with his foot bandaged and the water rough, he would surely drown if he were forced down. The minutes ticked by, the ship steaming to where they thought Blériot would be if he crashed. Nothing.

Then, suddenly, they heard cheering on the English coast. The Blériot XI had emerged from the clouds!

Shortly after five AM, Louis Blériot landed in a field with supporters waving the *Tricolore*, the French flag. His face was covered with oil that had been thrown from the engine. After being helped out of his airplane, he unstrapped his crutches and prepared to be escorted to a hero's welcome in London.

Library of Congress Prints and Photographs Division

Blériot in England.

Before he left, Blériot was told why Latham hadn't flown as well. In a supreme gesture of good sportsmanship, he agreed to split both the glory and the prize money if Latham would follow him across that day. But Blériot's luck was complete. Heavy wind and rain appeared almost as soon as he landed. Latham was left near Calais, "sitting with his head on his monoplane, weeping." Blériot was awarded the Legion of Honor and at a luncheon in his honor in London, he was handed his £1,000 check and proclaimed the greatest aviator in the world. The star-crossed Hubert Latham would try again weeks later, but once more his airplane could not make it across.

Part III

Higher, Steeper, Faster

Chapter 11

THE WEEK OF MIRACLES

Louis Blériot's conquest of the English Channel made France once again the center of world aviation. To celebrate their nation's glory, a group of champagne producers decided to host the world's first-ever "air meet" outside of Reims, about thirty miles east of Paris. Reims was the center of the Champagne region and also the site of a grand cathedral, with an interior larger than a football field and towers rising higher than a twenty-five-story building. For centuries, it was here that French kings had been crowned. In August 1909, Reims would see the crowning of the first kings of the skies.

The growers raised a good deal of money to sponsor what they called la Grande Semaine d'Aviation de la Champagne (the Great Aviation Week of Champagne). They paid to have railroad tracks laid from Paris to the fair site, with telephone and telegraph lines along the route. Grandstands were built that would seat thousands, and private luxury boxes would accommodate Europe's wealthy, famous, and noble. To make sure the elite had every comfort, private chefs, servants, and even hairdressers and florists were kept on call. For the actual flying, a six-mile course was laid out, and almost fifty sheds and airplane hangars were erected.

Tickets sold out almost as soon as they were printed. Within days, every hotel room in Reims was booked, and private home owners rented out spare bedrooms at high prices. Even that was not enough. City officials erected temporary shelters to house people who could not find other lodging. Eventually, so many spectators descended on Reims that an area large enough to hold forty thousand quickly had to be built next to the grandstand.

It had been only one year since Wilbur Wright had dazzled Europe with his flying, and now hundreds of thousands would flock to an air meet to see more than a dozen other flyers fight for glory in the air. Never before had so many come to one place to see this amazing new invention.

For those flyers, daily prizes and 200,000 francs would be awarded in a number of categories, including distance, speed, time in the air, and altitude. But the most important event would be the race for the Gordon Bennett Cup, named for an American newspaper publisher who had moved to Paris and was putting up the prize money. The winner would be the aviator who completed the fastest two laps of a ten-kilometer course, which was farther than any man had flown just one year before. France was betting on its new national hero, Louis Blériot.

The Wright brothers easily could have participated. Orville was already in Germany, trying to sell airplanes. He had dined with the German monarch Kaiser Wilhelm II, and his flying had awed the Germans as much as Wilbur's had amazed the French. But as they had with the Channel crossing, the Wright brothers declined the invitation to race at

Reims. They thought of events such as these as merely for show and not worth their time and effort.

With the Wright brothers unavailable, Glenn Curtiss was asked to represent the United States. Curtiss had moved on from balloons to fixed-wing aircraft, and he accepted instantly. Like Blériot, he was interested in the top prize, the Gordon Bennett Cup. He began working in secret to build an airplane that could beat Blériot and the other Europeans. "Without letting my plans become known to the public, I began at once to build an eight-cylinder, V-shaped, fifty horsepower motor. This was practically double the horsepower I had been using. Work on the motor was pushed day and night, as I had not an hour to spare."

Curtiss also designed a new frame for his airplane. He built it to be as small, light, and maneuverable as possible, and mounted a new invention called "ailerons" between the ends of the top and bottom wings. Ailerons, which mean "little wings," were an improvement on the Wright brothers' wing-warping method. These "little wings" would go up on one side and down on the other, which allowed Curtiss both to control his airplane and make very quick turns. They would also allow his racer to be more solidly built, since the bracing between the top and bottom wings could be more rigid. He called his entry the *Rheims Racer*.

Curtiss finished building his airplane with so little time to spare that "in order to get to Rheims in time to qualify, we had to take the aeroplane with us on the train as personal baggage." When he finally arrived at the meet, he was stunned to

Rheims or Reims?

Although "Rheims" was the accepted spelling in 1909, "Reims" is the common spelling today.

learn that Louis Blériot had mounted a powerful eight-cylinder, eighty-horsepower motor on his Blériot XI, and that Hubert Latham had been reported as flying at the unheard-of speed of sixty miles per hour. Curtiss then thought his chances "very slim indeed."

To make his chances even slimmer, Curtiss suffered a badly sprained ankle in a practice flight. Soon afterward, he barely avoided a midair collision with an Antoinette by quickly gaining altitude and flying over the other aircraft. The maneuver earned applause from the thousands who lined the practice area and a sigh of relief from

Library of Congress Prints and Photographs Division

Curtiss in the *Rheims Racer* on the left. The ailerons are the small attachments at the end of each wing.

Curtiss. His competitors had each brought two or three airplanes to the meet, but he had brought only one. If the *Rheims Racer* was damaged, he would be out of the competition. And he knew he was the only American flying before such celebrities as former first lady Edith Roosevelt, Teddy's wife, and eleven-year-old Quentin Roosevelt, the ex-president's youngest son.

And what a show they saw. The *New York Times* called the Reims meet "a week of miracles." Hundreds of thousands of men, women, and children who had never seen a plane in the air, many of whom did not even believe that flight was possible, witnessed three, five, even eight airplanes in the sky at once. On one occasion, seven aircraft flew in front of the immense, looming towers of the cathedral. The huge crowds gasped at crashes and cheered successes. Records for distance, time in the air, speed, and altitude—Latham soared to 508 feet—were beaten and then beaten again. One flyer stayed in the air for three hours and fourteen minutes, traveling 112.41 miles, beating Wilbur Wright's distance record—and winning $10,000 for himself.

But the great flying had taken a toll on the airplanes. By the time the Gordon Bennett Cup race was run, crashes and mechanical breakdowns had eliminated all but five qualifiers. Glenn Curtiss went first and, turning faster than any airplane had before, completed the course in 15 minutes, 50.4 seconds, or 45.73 miles per hour.

The next three flyers could not come close to Curtiss's time, but the last competitor was Blériot. With the more powerful engine, Blériot went faster than Curtiss on the straightaways but, using wing warping, was slower than the *Rheims Racer* on the turns. Still, Curtiss was certain Blériot had won. So were the spectators. The huge crowd began to chant Blériot's name and waited for officials to run the *Tricolore*

BLERIOT'S FLIGHT AT RHEIMS

Library of Congress Prints and Photographs Division

Blériot's flight at Reims.

up the flagpole to the strains of the French national anthem, "La Marseillaise."

But when officials ran up the flag of the winner, it was the Stars and Stripes! And what the band played was "The Star-Spangled Banner."

Curtiss had won! Blériot had finished six seconds behind.

Quentin Roosevelt

His father's favorite, Quentin would die in air combat in World War I, shot down over France on Bastille Day, 1918. He was twenty years old.

The two thousand Americans in the crowd cheered lustily, and Quentin Roosevelt told Curtiss his victory was "bully." With his victory, Glenn Curtiss had established himself as the fastest man in the air. On the last day of the meet, Curtiss won another speed race, this one thirty kilometers, and became, with Louis Blériot, one of the two most famous aviators in the world.

Chapter 12

A WEEK OF MIRACLES IN AMERICA

Since very few Americans had had the chance to see an airplane or an airship in flight, dirigibles remained popular. Baldwin, Knabenshue, and Beachey continued to tour the country with their dirigibles, drawing big crowds to see them race or soar together, making the giant gasbags seem to dance with one another in the air.

At a fair in St. Louis in October 1909, to mark the city's hundredth anniversary, balloonists were invited as the main attraction. After Glenn Curtiss's victory at Reims, however, the fair's organizers had set three days aside for Curtiss to fly his amazing fixed-wing airplane.

The balloons delighted the crowd perfectly well, but the spectators really went wild over Curtiss's flying. During their time together, Curtiss and Knabenshue talked about staging a major air meet in the United States, something like what the French had done at Reims. Baldwin and Beachey were excited about an American air meet as well. They decided to do it out west, where no fixed-wing airplane had yet flown. Knaben-shue suggested Los Angeles. It was then just a small but growing city, and local businessmen were interested in staging some grand event.

Not everyone who pushed the boundaries of aviation forward was a flyer. It would take the right kind of person to put on America's first-ever air meet, and Los Angeles had just the man. He was a local promoter named Dick Ferris, who had a nose for headlines and was known for bizarre stunts. He had produced everything from opera to automobile processions: He had staged plays with horses racing across the stage; he had even promoted a "nightinee," a nighttime baseball game between the Los Angeles Angels

DICK FERRIS

Dick Ferris.

and San Francisco Seals of the Pacific Coast League. Even better, he was also president of the local balloon club.

Ferris couldn't wait to get started. He spoke to the mayor, the city council, newspapermen, businessmen, bankers, and just about anyone else who could help pay for the meet, put up prize money, or get top flyers to travel across America. He contacted all the top aviators, including Blériot and Latham, promising them glory (and a lot of money) if they came to Los Angeles. Some were interested but wanted to be paid in advance; to them, Los Angeles was an outpost, and making one's way across America, even by railroad, was an expedition. The Wright brothers simply said no.

Ferris soon realized that even though he had money to spend, it would not be enough to attract many of the world's top aviators. He paid $10,000 to Curtiss, a necessity, since a star American had to be part of the show. With so hefty a fee, Curtiss promised to bring another aviator as well, someone he assured Ferris would amaze the crowd.

Of the invited Europeans, however, only Louis Paulhan agreed to come. Paulhan had been one of the most popular flyers at Reims and combined outstanding flying skills with European flair. He had set an altitude record that Latham had bested, and Los Angeles seemed the perfect place to reclaim his record. To get the Frenchman, however, Ferris had to pay $25,000, which, with Curtiss's $10,000, was almost his entire budget. He didn't have enough for anyone else.

It was a big risk. He was asking thousands and thousands of people to attend an event in which they believed that the world's best-known aviators would awe and amaze them. How would they react when the show consisted only of Glenn Curtiss, his mystery accomplice, and a Frenchman of whom no one in Los Angeles had heard?

But Dick Ferris was too experienced a promoter to let any doubt show in public. As the meet approached, he was in the papers almost every day, talking up the glories of his city and his air show. "I am in receipt of frequent telephone calls and written messages approving the idea as a great boost for Los Angeles, and in fact all California. It shows people the way to keep up with aeronautical progress nowadays and that we are not behind the rest of the world."

A Dick Ferris production.

His energy and his powers of persuasion were extraordinary. He found an excellent location, Dominguez Hill, a mesa south of central Los Angeles, and then convinced the owners to make the property available to him free of charge.

Ferris renamed the site Aviation Field and had a grandstand built that would hold twenty-five thousand people. A two-and-a-half-mile course was laid out, marked by towers, and an "aviation camp" of large tents was set up to house the airplanes and dirigibles. And this would not be *just* an air show. The meet would also feature a sideshow with carnival barkers and a variety of odd attractions. He raised $80,000 from local businessmen to be used only for prize money.

Just days before the meet, Glenn Curtiss revealed to the press that his other flyer was a thin, red-haired daredevil named Charles K. Hamilton, a man who always seemed to have a cigarette in his mouth and a drink in his hand. Ferris heaved a sigh of relief. Hamilton would most definitely be a draw. He had begun in balloons, but they were not exciting enough for him. He seemed to be happy only when he was risking his life.

In the weeks before the Los Angeles air show, Hamilton had flown in a gale wind, then in a blinding snowstorm; won a race against an electric automobile; sped across the sky at a record-breaking 62.72 miles per hour; crashed twice; barely missed telegraph wires another time; and once had to dive from his airplane as it skidded across the ice, landing face-first on a frozen lake. No aviator in history would have more crashes—sixty-three—and survive them all. Charley

Charles K. Hamilton.

Hamilton crashed in dirigibles, gliders, and fixed-wing airplanes. He regularly emerged from exhibitions bloodied, bruised, and with broken bones. The crowds quickly grew to the thousands to watch this man who seemed to have no fear of death, and who could escape any situation with his life. They loved him.

Even with just Curtiss, Hamilton, and the Frenchman Paulhan, Dick Ferris sold tickets as far up the Pacific coast as Seattle. It seemed certain that attendance for the ten-day event would reach 250,000.

Other than what those three would fly, however, the rest of the fixed-wing airplanes were an odd group, giving a strong sense of just how new *real* aviation was. One was a bizarre, five-winged creation built by a

Ornithopters

Wing-flapping devices were called "ornithopters." Although many inventors had tried, no one had ever been able to get one to fly.

science teacher at Los Angeles Polytechnic High School. Another was a contraption in which the aviator tried to fly by flapping artificial wings, built by a different teacher from the same school.

Opening day arrived and it was instantly clear that the Los Angeles air meet would be every bit as important in inspiring the American public's thirst for flying as Reims had been for Europe. Curtiss made the opening flight, "soaring like a huge bird," and became the first man ever to fly an airplane on the Pacific coast. The crowd waited for Charles Hamilton to do something amazing, but it was Paulhan who took their breath away. The Frenchman had arrived in Los Angeles in a special railroad car with his wife, his business manager, two other French aviators, eight mechanics, and a poodle named Escapade. He made three flights that first day, the last almost thirty miles. He gave "a remarkable exhibition of control over his machine, gracefully making sharp turns, dipping almost to the ground, scattering a group of frightened officers, and skimming over the grandstand only a few feet above the heads of the spectators." After a perfect landing, "Paulhan was cheered madly. Men shouted themselves hoarse while women applauded and waved handkerchiefs. Paulhan danced gaily into his tent."

The next day, and for the remainder of the meet, Paulhan, Curtiss, and Hamilton dazzled spectators with flying that most would not have thought possible. "Here, on historic ground," a reporter raved, "world's records were broken and cross-country flights were undertaken that

Library of Congress Prints and Photographs Division

Louis Paulhan flies to 4,164 feet.

demonstrated beyond the question of a doubt the practicability of the aeroplane." Among the many highlights: Curtiss flew fifty-five miles per hour with a passenger; Paulhan took up an army officer, who dropped sandbags as pretend "bombs"; Paulhan, Curtiss, and Hamilton took off and flew together as a squadron; aviators chased one another around the field, dipping and diving over the grandstand; Paulhan set an altitude record by flying to 4,164 feet—1,000 feet higher than Hubert Latham had ascended in Europe just a few days before. It was an amazing height, considering that just four months earlier, Latham had set an official record of five hundred feet. Paulhan stunned the spectators by flying off to a nearby racetrack and then returning, a distance of forty-five miles. He won $10,000 for the longest flight. Later, he made a twenty-mile flight

over the Pacific with his wife in the passenger seat, and then took Dick
Ferris, Mrs. Ferris, and other celebrities up as passengers.

On the final day, Curtiss and Paulhan staged a sort of duel. Paulhan
was flying for the endurance prize—time in the air—while Curtiss was
flying for speed. Paulhan started first in a Blériot monoplane and Curtiss,
back in the *Rheims Racer*, took off after him. By the third lap, Curtiss had
caught up, the two airplanes coming over the grandstand "with the speed
of express trains." Curtiss easily won the prize for speed, as well as for
quick starts, turning, and perfect landings, but Paulhan won for altitude,
endurance, and cross-country flying. In the end, Paulhan won $19,000 in
prize money, and the Curtiss team won slightly more than $10,000.

When the meet closed, the flyers received hundreds of exhibition
requests. The next day, Paulhan departed for a tour that would take him
first to San Francisco and then east with stops all through the southern

Library of Congress: Chronicling America

Balloon race at Los Angeles.

half of the United States. Hamilton took the *Rheims Racer* to San Diego and up the California coast to Oregon and Washington to continue cheating death with his flying. In Seattle, he dived straight down from three hundred feet, aiming at a pond. His idea was to skim the airplane along the surface and then take off again. Instead, one of his wingtips touched the water and the airplane "turned a somersault and fell, a mass of wreckage, into the water." Hamilton did not break any bones this time, but he collapsed just after he was rescued, and was taken to the hospital with a serious head injury. He was back in the air within a week.

At stop after stop, the crowds gathered and cheered. Fixed-wing flying had conquered the west.

Beachey and Knabenshue had performed wonderfully in Los Angeles as well. They soared together and showed incredible control of the giant balloons. Beachey won the dirigible race and Knabenshue finished second. But although newspapers reported that "the spectators were thrilled," Beachey could tell that the public would not be thrilled by dirigibles much longer. Lincoln Beachey once again looked into the future and decided on the spot that he must move to fixed-wing aircraft.

Chapter 13

THE STARDUST TWINS

After Los Angeles, the Wright brothers realized that their plans to sell airplanes without tapping into the growing public frenzy with aviation would not work—they had to get into exhibition flying. They hired Roy Knabenshue to put together a team. The first thing Knabenshue did was offer Lincoln Beachey a place. Beachey had never flown a fixed-wing aircraft, but that didn't stop him from asking for more money than the fifty dollars per day that Wilbur and Orville had offered to pay. When Knabenshue told Orville that Beachey wanted hundreds, perhaps as much as a thousand dollars to fly, Orville wouldn't hear of it. He also refused to employ Charley Hamilton, whose smoking and drinking he found offensive.

Orville and Wilbur were convinced they didn't need Beachey or Hamilton. The growing obsession with aviation was not simply among those who wanted to watch airplanes fly but also among those who wanted to fly them. By May 1910, twenty-five men had applied to join the Wright team. Some were from close to home, such as Walter Brookins, a local boy who had known the Wright family while growing up. Others came from farther away, such as Californians Arch Hoxsey, an automobile racer, and bicycle trick rider Ralph Johnstone. Neither Hoxsey nor Johnstone had ever flown before, but in those days, few men had.

After watching Paulhan, Hamilton, and Curtiss at Los Angeles, Hoxsey decided to change careers. "All Hoxsey could talk about was the air meet," a friend said later. "He said, 'Did you hear about the prizes? My heavens, they give $10,000 for a prize. I don't think it would be any harder to fly those things than to drive a racing car. That's for me.' Things worked fast in those days, and within a few months, he was the Wright brothers' top flyer."

But being a flyer for the Wrights did not mean getting rich. A member

Arch Hoxsey and his passenger, former president Theodore Roosevelt.

of the Wright team told what it was like to fly for Wilbur and Orville. "They sent us all over the country…to make money for the Wrights. They gave us a base salary of $20 a week, and $50 a day for every day we flew." The Wrights were receiving $1,000 per day for each aviator who performed, so the exhibition flyers made them a lot of money. The Wrights were very religious, and team members were forbidden to drink, smoke, or swear, and there was no flying on Sunday. Curtiss flyers did much better—he split fifty-fifty with anyone who flew a Curtiss airplane, and put fewer restrictions on his employees.

The Wright team members might not have made as much money as the Curtiss flyers, but they did become famous. Arch Hoxsey took the governor of New Jersey up for a flight, as well as former president Theodore Roosevelt. On August 19, 1910, he and Ralph Johnstone flew at night, becoming the first people in the United States to do so. At show after show, they soared long and gracefully before adoring crowds.

But flying still had its dark side. In 1910, no one tested airplanes before they flew in exhibitions. The exhibitions *were* the tests. That meant flyers were always risking their own lives and sometimes the lives of those who had come to watch them. In August 1910, Walter Brookins crashed when photographers crowding the field made him change his landing and he lost control in high winds. Heading directly toward the spectators, Brookins swerved at the last moment, missing the grandstand by a foot, and crashed in an alley crowded with workers, policemen, and soldiers. He had put his own life in peril to save others, and his flying saved many spectators. But ten people were caught under the crushed airplane, with one boy suffering a fractured skull and another a broken arm. Brookins himself was first reported as killed, though he suffered only bruises and a broken nose.

But people pay to see danger. The accident was said to double admissions sales the following day.

Arch Hoxsey and Ralph Johnstone came to understand early on that the more dangerously they flew, the more people would pay to see them. They became known as the "Stardust Twins" for their constant attempts to best the altitude marks of the other. At one meet at Belmont Park in New York, in October 1910, which boasted possibly the greatest group of flyers ever assembled, they would fly a duel that would send Ralph Johnstone to a then-unheard-of seven thousand feet into the air. Neither man would have believed that after such a remarkable achievement, a different aviator would be the meet's biggest star.

That aviator, after flying for less than four months, had amazed onlookers in France with flying that was either brilliant or insanely reckless—no one could ever be sure.

Chapter 14

AMERICAN HERO

Among the two thousand Americans who watched Glenn Curtiss fly to victory in the Gordon Bennett Cup at Reims in September 1909 was Joseph Jean Baptiste Moisant, the fourth and youngest son of French Canadian parents who had emigrated from Quebec to Illinois. Proud to be American, the boys had changed their names, and so "Joseph Jean Baptiste" became "John Bevins." When he went to see Curtiss fly at Reims, John Bevins Moisant was already an international celebrity. Just months before, he had evaded capture and possible execution after a third attempt to lead an invasion of El Salvador.

Invading a foreign country was not out of character for the amazing Moisant family. They had left Illinois for California in the 1880s and within ten years had made a fortune in lumber, real estate, and mining. In 1895, John's oldest brother, Alfred, bought a sugarcane plantation in

El Salvador so large that it took an entire day to ride from one end to the other. He also bought a salt mine and a bank.

For more than ten years, the Moisants made huge profits in Central America, helped by Alfred's "donating" large amounts of money to keep the governments friendly. (Bribery was illegal but common practice when Alfred was making his fortune. In fact, without paying government officials, it was impossible to do business.) In 1907, however, General Fernando Figueroa took power in El Salvador. He owed a good deal of money to Alfred's bank and decided he did not want to pay it back. He demanded the Moisants forgive the loan—mark it as paid—and "donate" some of their sugar plantation to the government, meaning him. Alfred Moisant was willing to negotiate, but John decided only direct action would do. John recruited others in Central America who hated Figueroa and planned an attack from the sea. On June 11, 1907, John's army landed on a beach near the Moisant plantation, guns blazing. The battle began well for the invaders, but then some of the men John had recruited began to argue about who would run the country after Figueroa had been kicked out. With Moisant's officers fighting among themselves, Figueroa's soldiers were able to turn the battle their way. John was forced to leap onto a boat to escape.

But John Moisant did not give up. For two more years, he plotted and sometimes attacked; he was jailed, hunted, and threatened by both Figueroa and the United States government. Some saw him as a rogue and others as a swashbuckling hero. He attempted two more invasions, the second in April 1909, five months before the race at Reims. This time, his forces were intercepted by United States Navy warships. They threatened to fire on him if he attempted to land. Moisant steamed away, escaping arrest and imprisonment by his own government. With John in hiding, Alfred spent weeks talking with officials in Washington, DC. They finally agreed to let John return home if he agreed never to be involved in politics again—anyone's politics. In July 1909, John stepped off an ocean liner in New York a free man.

Free, perhaps, but desperate for something to do. On a whim, he traveled to Reims to watch the meet and instantly decided that exhibition flying was exactly what he had been looking for.

John Moisant threw himself into aviation. His plan was to become the world's greatest exhibition flyer in an aircraft of his own creation. Along with his sister Matilde, he observed birds in flight. Then, before he had ever flown himself, he set to designing and building an airplane. It was typical of the Moisants that stuffy, conservative Alfred fully supported his younger brother's plan and gave him all the money he needed to carry it out.

Light Metals

How strong something is compared to its weight is called a "weight-to-strength ratio." The aim, of course, is to make something as light as possible without sacrificing strength. Aluminum, especially when combined with other metals in "alloys," was perfect for the job.

John had spoken French since he was a child, so working in France wouldn't be a problem. He set up shop near Paris and began to craft his airplane. He was convinced that his design should be as light and strong as possible. So instead of using wood, he built the world's first airplane made entirely of metal, mostly aluminum. He also employed a new engine, the Gnome, which was very powerful and spun with the propeller around a crankshaft that didn't move. Best of all, it weighed only 176 pounds.

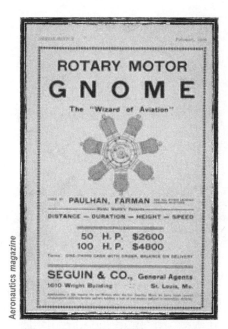

Aeronautics *magazine*

Magazine ad for a Gnome motor.

He called his invention an "aluminoplane," and named it *L'Ecrevisse* ("The Crayfish"). Then, without bothering to take a single flying lesson, John Moisant seated himself behind the engine, signaled his mechanic to start the engine, and lifted off. His Crayfish performed wonderfully...too wonderfully. *L'Ecrevisse* shot into the sky and climbed at a steep angle—at speeds approaching eighty miles per hour. It was faster than anyone had flown before. That was too high, too fast, even for Moisant. Faced with an almost certain high-speed crash, he cut his engine. *L'Ecrevisse* turned nose down and returned almost straight to its starting point.

Incredibly, Moisant wasn't hurt in the crash, though his airplane was ruined. He immediately started on another, but this time took some flying lessons from Louis Blériot before venturing once more into the skies. Moisant's second airplane, *Le Corbeau* ("The Crow"), did not do much better than the first. He gave up designing, bought a Blériot, and turned his attention solely to flying.

Moisant's Design

Further examination revealed that *L'Ecrevisse* was capable of sustaining flight—John Moisant had successfully designed an airplane with no training or experience.

Moisant's *Le Corbeau*.

John B. Moisant burst on the aviation scene like a comet. When the French refused to allow "the crazy American kid" to fly in Le Circuit de l'Est, the world's first long-distance air race, Moisant packed his friend Roland Garros into the passenger seat of his Blériot and flew thirty-seven miles across Paris, passing directly over the Eiffel Tower, and then landed on the field where a quarter million people had shown up to see the event begin. Moisant told reporters who gathered around him that flying into the grounds was the only way he could watch the race. Then, to further thrust himself into the spotlight, he announced that he intended to fly from Paris to London and that he would take his mechanic along—the first time anyone crossed the Channel with a passenger.

To many, the idea seemed idiotic—Moisant was only 140 pounds, but the mechanic weighed 185 pounds, and 325 pounds was much too heavy for the Blériot. Louis Blériot himself begged Moisant not to attempt the crossing.

But the mechanic told Moisant that Blériot was wrong—the airplane was stronger than the man who had built it thought it was. On August 16,

1910, John B. Moisant took off from Paris with only an ordinary compass for navigation. There were clouds and fog the entire trip—if Moisant took a single incorrect reading on the compass, his airplane could run out of fuel over the Channel and crash.

But Moisant's readings were true. One day and three stops in the French countryside later, John Moisant, his hands numb from the cold, touched down with his mechanic on the English side, six miles from Dover. The

Roland Garros

Garros would become a famed exhibition flyer in his own right. When France entered World War I, he became one of its best pilots, but was killed in combat during the last days of the war. The tennis stadium where the French Open is played is named in his honor.

next morning, the pair left for London. This last leg was to be made with an additional passenger—a cat given to Moisant by an English engineer, which Moisant named Paree-Londres. The Dover-to-London run was plagued by breakdowns, bad weather, and other delays, but finally, on

September 6, Moisant and his mechanic completed the journey. Within days, he was invited to fly in an upcoming air meet at Belmont Park, in New York. Moisant accepted, intending by meet's end to be hailed as the greatest flyer in the world.

John Moisant and Paree-Londres.

Chapter 15

THE WORLD COMES TO NEW YORK

In 1910, New York was the largest, richest, and most famous city in the United States, and the only one considered the equal of the great capitals of Europe. The Belmont meet promised to be a spectacle worthy of the city's reputation, and the daring and brilliance of its flyers would be reported on the front pages of newspapers across America.

The roster was, by far, the most impressive ever assembled. Among those competing for prizes were Hubert Latham, Charles K. Hamilton, Walter Brookins, Arch Hoxsey, Ralph Johnstone, Roland Garros, a brilliant British flyer named Claude Grahame-White…and Cap't Tom Baldwin, who had switched from dirigibles to fixed-wing craft and brought his own biplane.

There were dozens of prizes and almost $70,000 in prize money. At first, it seemed that the most important race would be for the 1910 Gordon Bennett Cup. But it turned out that the Gordon Bennett race was not to be the only important prize that was awarded. A separate $10,000 prize was offered to the winner of a race from the fairgrounds at Belmont Park—near where John F. Kennedy International Airport is today— around the Statue of Liberty and back, a race that would be viewed by more people than had ever seen an airplane before.

Newspapers immediately played up the Statue of Liberty race as the most important and most difficult ever flown. To get to the Statue of Liberty from Belmont Park meant flying across Brooklyn, where a direct route would take a flyer over the rooftops of one of the most densely populated areas in the entire United States. There would be no place to land in an emergency; no way to recover if a downdraft pulled the airplane to earth. Engine trouble meant almost certain death for the aviator and probably some people on the ground. Very few flyers, aviation experts predicted, would be brave—or foolhardy—enough to enter.

But one who would, to nobody's surprise, would be John Bevins Moisant. He stepped off the boat in New York and announced he would enter the Statue of Liberty race and that he expected to win. His Paris-London flight had made him a folk hero. He was small, handsome, and charming, and stressed in interviews that he would be flying for America. He was a reporter's dream.

As the opening of the meet grew near, hundreds of thousands of tickets were sold. People wondered if the event could possibly live up to its advance billing. They needn't have been concerned. Before the meet closed on October 30, nearly every important world record would be broken and then broken again. It could rightly be said that those eight days in New York changed aviation from a curiosity—a fad—to one of the great social movements in history.

Library of Congress Prints and Photographs Division

Planes in the air at Belmont.

Determining Altitude

Altitude was measured with a "barograph," a barometer mounted on the airplane where variations in atmospheric pressure were recorded on a paper mounted on a revolving drum. By comparing the changes from readings on the ground and then correcting for other factors, such as humidity, a good approximation of altitude could be obtained.

It did not begin that way, however. On opening day, October 22, a driving rain drenched the course. Still, tens of thousands of spectators showed up to watch seven airplanes fly. Ten were in the sky at once just two days later. That same day, J. Armstrong "Chip" Drexel, an American flying a Blériot, set an altitude record of 7,183 feet. The press called it the "greatest day's flying seen in the United States since the Wright brothers," an accolade that would not last twenty-four hours.

The following afternoon saw one of the greatest air duels in history. Ralph Johnstone, Arch Hoxsey, Hubert Latham, and France's Count Jacques de Lesseps took off, intending to break Drexel's record. At about five thousand feet, Latham suddenly began to dive, swinging side to side in swirling air as he tried desperately to maintain control. When his airplane disappeared behind a clump of trees, there were gasps from the crowd. Many were convinced that Latham had crashed and died. But Latham landed his airplane—even if he didn't quite know how he had managed it—and walked out from the trees uninjured.

Ralph Johnstone.

Aircraft *magazine*

Hoxsey and de Lesseps continued to climb, but each had to break off the chase at about seven thousand feet because of the wind and frigid weather. But Johnstone kept going, flying through the clouds and a "raging snowstorm." He climbed higher and higher, snow and hail whipping across his airplane and frost fogging his goggles. When he finally returned to earth, officials announced that he had soared to 7,303 feet.

One day after that, Johnstone and Hoxsey "went up in a gale so stiff that for a time they hung over the field immobile, though they were steadily gaining in altitude, and then began to drift backward." Johnstone was blown fifty miles out over Long Island. It was the only occasion in aviation history that airplanes were seen to fly in reverse. It was remarkable that Johnstone and Hoxsey could keep control under such conditions.

Johnstone saved his most impressive achievement for the end. Altitude records were smashed at Belmont almost daily. Johnstone flew the highest—an unheard-of 9,714 feet.

The exploits of the Stardust Twins had set the stage for the Gordon Bennett race, scheduled for the morning of October 29. The Liberty run was supposed to take place later the same day, but delays forced it back to the afternoon of October 30. The favorites in the Gordon Bennett race were Claude Grahame-White in a Blériot with a 100-horsepower Gnome motor, and Walter Brookins in the Wright R, a racing airplane Wilbur and Orville had designed especially for this race. In practice runs, it had exceeded eighty miles per hour.

Just after taking off, however, but before Brookins's start could be

Claude Grahame-White.

declared official, four of the eight cylinders on the Wright R failed. Brookins tried to control the craft in a twenty-mile-per-hour tailwind, but the airplane plunged to the ground not fifty feet from the grandstand. Brookins was thrown from the machine in great pain, his "whole body black and blue, as though he had been beaten with a club," but once again he had escaped without serious injury.

With Brookins out, Grahame-White tore through the twenty-lap, 62.1-mile course in one hour and one minute, beating the "mile-a-minute" mark, faster than anyone had ever flown such a distance. Neither of the other two Americans, Charles Hamilton nor Chip Drexel, were able even to approach Grahame-White's time. But with Brookins not having officially run, a spot had opened up on the three-man American team, a perfect opportunity for a daring aviator to be thrust into the breach to save America's honor.

John B. Moisant.

Hamilton's manager rushed to the hangars to urge Moisant to fly. He was America's only chance. Moisant, eating a piece of pie, said that his airplane had been damaged in an earlier crash and was not yet fully repaired. The controlling mechanism would not allow him to maneuver properly and might even cause a crash. The manager begged Moisant to fly anyway and told him that he must do so immediately or the deadline to begin would pass. Moisant, "between mouthfuls of pie," hurried into his aviation clothes and ordered his damaged Blériot out of the hangar.

With literally seconds to spare before the race was closed, Moisant took off. He completed only six laps before his shoulders and arms were shaking so badly from the effort of controlling the damaged machine that he was forced to land. Mechanics worked quickly to try to make the airplane handle more easily. Once again just beating the clock, Moisant took off and completed the final fourteen laps. While Grahame-White's time was never in danger—he won by almost an hour—Moisant astounded spectators and his fellow flyers alike by finishing second.

When Moisant taxied to a halt, he was all but dragged by American officials into the clubhouse, where he was cheered and toasted with champagne. In the newspapers the next day, Moisant's second-place finish was treated as heroic.

The Statue of Liberty race began the following afternoon. As expected, few of the flyers were willing to fly a course in which the chance of tragedy was so great. Grahame-White was one of the brave (or foolish) few, and another was Count de Lesseps. Charles Hamilton entered but his airplane would not start. The final contestant was John Moisant.

Seventy-five thousand spectators cheered when de Lesseps took to the air just after three PM, and Grahame-White followed three minutes later. Moisant wheeled out his Blériot, climbed aboard, and signaled his mechanic to start the motor. When the engine turned over, instead of taxiing, the aircraft spun on the ground and crashed into another airplane. Moisant's rudder had jammed and his Blériot was left with a wing damaged beyond repair.

Moisant sat stunned in his doomed monoplane. His plans to become the meet's most acclaimed aviator seemed hopeless. What terrible luck! The crash that had damaged his airplane had prevented him from running in earlier events. The second-place finish in the Gordon Bennett, although it garnered him great praise, was still, well, second. And now, in the most important event of the entire meet, he would not even get to compete.

With John just sitting in his airplane, his brother Alfred hurried over

Aircraft magazine

Gordon Bennett trophy. The airplane is a Wright Flyer, even though the Wright brothers never competed in a Gordon Bennett race.

to find out if he was hurt. When he learned that John was fine, Alfred told him to get out of the wreck. They would buy another airplane. They jumped into Alfred's automobile and raced through the grounds. Eventually, they came upon a new fifty-horse-power Blériot belonging to another French aviator who had crashed a different plane during the Gordon Bennett race and was in his Manhattan hotel bed, injured. Albert telephoned and offered the man $10,000 for his airplane. The French aviator accepted instantly (the Blériot had cost him, at most, $1,500).

As John's newly purchased monoplane was being prepared, two tiny dots appeared in the west. The first was Grahame-White, who had taken a northern route to avoid some of the more densely populated areas. Behind him was de Lesseps, who had swung to the south, where some emergency landing spots were located. Grahame-White completed the thirty-six-mile race in thirty-five minutes and twenty-one seconds, got out of the cockpit, swept off his hat and goggles, and bowed to the crowd as the band played "God Save the

King." De Lesseps landed five minutes later to the strains of "La Marseillaise." Moisant had yet to take off.

The crowd, rather than cheer the winner, began to chant Moisant's name as an airplane he had never as much as set foot in was wheeled out. Leaving a furious Grahame-White to stand and watch, Moisant's newly purchased Blériot left the ground at 4:06.

As many as one million people watched along the route—in roads, on rooftops, in boats, or along the edge of the harbor. A reporter for the *New York Times*, watching from near the Statue of Liberty, later wrote of the strange lack of noise from the huge crowd "as each minute speck in the sky grew into a clearly visible man in a flying machine." It was one of the most vivid descriptions of the public's reaction to early air travel ever put to paper. "The sight, at first uncanny, held them speechless. Cold chills ran down the back. In spite of the fact that they all knew about aeroplanes and that they really do fly, seeing one do it was something like meeting a ghost."

Grahame-White's machine was more powerful, but Moisant simply refused to be denied the prize. He had been given a second chance and did not intend to waste it. He threw aside all caution and headed directly for Bedloe's Island, barely clearing treetops and buildings in the most populated section of the route. As he approached the Statue, he climbed to three thousand feet, then made his turn for home. Moisant retraced that same direct route back to the finish and beat Grahame-White's time by forty-two seconds. Later, when his sister Matilde was asked about John's having chosen a flight path without any chance of an emergency landing, she replied, "My brother doesn't fly to land. He flies to win."

As soon as Moisant was declared the winner, Grahame-White stormed over to the judges' table. He accused them of cheating him by allowing

Moisant to start late, because they wanted an American to win. He filed an official protest and then asked to repeat his run, so that he too could fly directly at the statue. With an engine of twice the power, he would have no trouble recording a winning time. The judges went "long into the night" before denying Grahame-White a second chance.

The Statue of Liberty flight made John Moisant not just the story of the meet but the *American* story. A reporter wrote, "Moisant, his face red from the fanning of the cold air, shouted too, demanding cheers not for himself, but for America. The band struck into 'The Star-Spangled Banner' and the crowd cheered. It switched to 'Yankee Doodle' and yells greeted it. There were tears in the cheers and there were sobs in the shouts of every man, woman, and child who had seen Moisant's return, for something was welling up that made them want to cry for sheer happiness."

This was quite a change for a man who had been declared a fugitive from justice by his own government not six months before.

Aeronautics magazine

John Moisant circling the Statue of Liberty.

Chapter 16

A WOMAN'S PLACE
IS IN THE AIR

With his brother now one of the most famous men in America, Alfred Moisant decided aviation would be good business as well as good sport. Only days after the Belmont meet, he formed a company, Moisant International Aviators, Inc., committing $750,000 of his own money to cover expenses (nearly $20 million in today's money). His plan included a "flying circus," a traveling airborne spectacle with his brother John as the main attraction, as well as a flying school. The Moisant Aviation School didn't open until the following year. When it did, the first two students to sign up guaranteed that the school would receive wide coverage in the press.

Both were women.

Women could not vote then, and most were expected to content themselves with tending to the cooking, the cleaning, and their

June, 1911 AIRCRAFT 127

The Hempstead Plains Aviation Co.

Announces the

OPENING

OF THE

MOISANT AVIATION SCHOOL

At Garden City, L. I., N. Y.

Under the personal direction of

ALFRED J. MOISANT

Assisted by

Roland G. Garros	St. Croix Johnstone
René Simon	Edmond Audemars
René Barrier	Andrew Houpert

The finest flying grounds in America, hundreds of acres without an obstruction, only eighteen miles from New York City, and a two and one-half mile straightaway

French Pilot-Aviators are the Instructors

Flying is a Fine Sport, a Splendid Science
and a Rich Livelihood

LEARN HOW TO FLY

FOR FULL PARTICULARS ADDRESS

ALFRED J. MOISANT, President - TIMES BUILDING, NEW YORK

Moisant Aviation School ad.

children. "A woman's place is in the home," the popular saying went. Women who defied that convention—and there were many, including race-car drivers, explorers, artists, and writers—were admired by some and hated by others. They were often subject to public abuse and demands that they return to their "traditional" place. Most refused. Those women, who would not conform to the roles society had laid out for them, helped change the way in which all women in American society were viewed—and are viewed today. That was especially true in flying. In taking to perhaps the most dangerous, romantic, and *modern* of activities, women aviators enhanced both flying and respect for their gender.

The first of these two students was John's sister Matilde. Small and vivacious, Matilde wanted to fly since she had studied birds with her brother John. In most families, of course, a woman would be forbidden from pursuing something as "male" as flying, or at least dissuaded. But the Moisants, as they proved again and again, were not like most families. Matilde was not only allowed to fly, she was encouraged to.

The second student was one of the most extraordinary women ever to take to the skies. She blazed a trail for every woman who believed she could achieve her dreams, not just in the air but in whatever arena she wished to compete. Her name was Harriet Quimby.

A stunning beauty, tall and sleek, described by Matilde Moisant as "the prettiest girl I've ever seen,"

Matilde Moisant.

National Air and Space Museum Archives, Smithsonian Institution

Harriet Quimby was a feature writer at a popular magazine called *Leslie's Illustrated Weekly*. In autumn 1910, *Leslie's* planned to devote an entire issue to aviation, and Quimby persuaded her editor to send her to Belmont. There she met the Moisants and struck up friendships with John and Matilde.

Quimby was thirty-five at the time but looked ten years younger. She had been born in rural Michigan in May 1875, but her father lost his

Harriet Quimby in her flying suit.

farm and the family moved west to San Francisco. Her mother later claimed that the family was of proper New England stock, a fiction that Harriet was happy to adopt as she made her way in the world.

When she reached her early twenties, Quimby decided to be an actress. She met another woman, Linda Arvidson, who also wanted a career on the stage, but they had no luck getting work. So the two women raised forty dollars to rent a theater and put on a musical show. Half the money came from San Francisco mayor James Phelan, who fell for a tale of woe from two beautiful young actresses. Quimby was so striking that a stage photographer took her picture free of charge for the window display, and local merchants lent them rugs and furniture. According to Arvidson, they received "good notices, but not enough to help our careers."

Arvidson continued to try to get acting work, but Quimby quit the stage and found work as a feature writer for a newspaper, the

San Francisco Call, where she wrote such articles as "Behind the Scenes with Bernhardt." She also published articles about art and theater.

In 1903, Quimby left San Francisco for New York and was hired by *Leslie's Illustrated Weekly*. For the next seven years, she wrote theater reviews, and articles on everything from businesses that operate underground to the effects of color on human behavior to alligator nests in Florida to fortune-tellers in Egypt. Her pieces were picked up by newspapers across America.

Sarah Bernhardt

"The Divine Sarah," born in Paris, was the most famous actress of her day. She was known for brilliant performances in a variety of roles, some of them quite scandalous for that time. She eventually starred in a number of silent movies, continuing to act until her death at age seventy-eight in 1923.

D. W. Griffith

D. W. Griffith is generally thought to be one of greatest—and most controversial—film directors of all time. His masterpiece, *Birth of a Nation*, is brilliant in its camera shots and production values and is taught at film schools around the world. But Griffith was a terrible racist, and the content of the film, which glorifies the Ku Klux Klan, is repugnant.

Linda Arvidson remained in the West. During a play called *Miss Petticoats*, she met a young actor who called himself Lawrence Griffith, although his real first name was David. Griffith was the son of a Confederate colonel who had fought with Stonewall Jackson. The two were married and the next year, Griffith came east, intending to be a playwright.

When he arrived, however, he took up film directing instead. At his wife's suggestion, Griffith began to be known by his initials, D. W.

In 1909, Harriet Quimby appeared in a short film directed by Griffith called *Lines of White on a Sullen Sea*. Quimby had a small part as a "fisher-maiden"; two of her fellow bit players were Mack Sennett and Mary Pickford.

Quimby did not appear in any more films but did write screenplays for shorts, five of which were filmed by Griffith and produced by the Biograph Company in 1911. Quimby gave her scripts such exotic titles as *The Blind Princess and the Poet*, *Sunshine Through the Dark*, and *His Mother's Scarf*.

Stage and Screen

Mack Sennett would later be known as the father of slapstick comedy, with his most famous creation the bumbling Keystone Cops. Mary Pickford went on to be one of the most famous of the silent film actresses and, with her husband, Douglas Fairbanks, was one of the founders of the United Artists film studio.

At Belmont, when Quimby announced her desire to learn to fly, John thought it an excellent idea. When the school opened, Quimby persuaded her editor to pay the $750 fee, promising him a terrific story.

On August 1, 1911, Harriet Quimby passed the test given by the Aero Club and won license 37, becoming the first woman to be a licensed flyer in the United States. Twelve days later, Matilde was granted license 44.

By the same time the following year, Harriet Quimby would be one of the most famous women in the world.

Chapter 17

FLYING FOR THE NAVY

In 1910, a nation's prestige was often determined by the strength of its navy. Great Britain, a relatively small country, maintained an empire that stretched around the world due mainly to its dominance on the high seas. With aviation so new, few believed airpower would replace sea power, but there were those who insisted that air power *combined* with sea power could greatly add to America's military might.

From the time he first began experimenting with fixed-wing aircraft, Glenn Curtiss had been fascinated with the possibilities of airplanes on the water. One day, an editor at the *New York World* asked if it would be possible "to launch an aeroplane from the deck of a ship at sea and have it fly back to shore carrying messages."

Curtiss set to work and had soon drawn up a plan to build an airplane runway on a regular steamship. There was great excitement at the idea, and a cruise-ship company offered one of its ocean liners for the test on a scheduled voyage to Europe. "The ship was fitted with a large platform erected on the stern," Curtiss said, "a platform sloping downward, and wide enough to allow an aeroplane set up on it to run down so that it could gather headway for its flight. The plan was to take the aeroplane fifty miles out to sea on the outward voyage from New York, and then launch it from the platform."

But the flight never came off, first because of bad weather and then because of a cracked propeller. The ship was forced to sail before repairs on the airplane could be completed.

But a naval officer named Washington Irving Chambers, who had been at Belmont, persuaded the navy to offer the cruiser *Birmingham* for Curtiss's test. Curtiss traveled to Norfolk, Virginia, and built his fifty-seven-foot, downward-sloping platform over the bow. A young aviator named Eugene Ely asked to fly the airplane.

Ely was an Iowa farm boy who had moved to San Francisco at age eighteen. He was fascinated with automobiles and worked as a mechanic, a salesman, a chauffeur, and finally as a race-car driver. As a twenty-year-old, Ely had drawn praise during the great 1906 earthquake for three times risking his life by driving through raging fires to rescue hospital patients. The next year, he married a high school principal's daughter and moved to Oregon, where he discovered that he liked flying even more than driving. With his wife, Mabel, as his manager, Ely began to appear at exhibitions and Curtiss signed him up.

Curtiss and Ely waited for good weather, but early winter storms set in and lasted for days. Finally, on November 14, 1910, Ely insisted on making the try. He waited for the sleet to clear, and then in rain, wind, and fog—terrible conditions—Ely took off from the *Birmingham*'s deck. His airplane could not build up enough speed on the short runway and it dropped just after it cleared the end of the platform. Ely barely avoided crashing into the sea thirty-seven feet below. As it was, his wheels touched the water and sent up a spray that damaged the propeller and drenched Ely, covering his goggles. He regained some altitude but found himself surrounded by fog, unsure of his location or in which direction he was going.

Eugene Ely.

Ely glanced around frantically, trying to figure out where to fly. He first headed out to sea, where he would surely have died—Ely could not swim—but, almost by instinct, he realized his error and turned back. Still, surrounded by fog, he could not be certain he had made the correct decision. But he kept flying, hoping for the fog to clear. Finally it did, just long enough for Ely to see that he was near a beach. He descended quickly, before the fog could once more close around him. Weather conditions stayed clear just long enough for Ely to land on the beach "within a few yards of the Hampton Roads Yacht Club house." He had flown five miles in five minutes.

Ely had made himself a star—and also won a prize of $5,000 for the first flight of at least one mile from a ship to land.

Aeronautics magazine

Ely taking off from the *Birmingham*.

With the triumphs at Belmont and Ely's flight from a warship, aviation seemed ready for a great leap forward. Then, on November 16, 1910, at an air show in Denver, Ralph Johnstone, one of the Stardust Twins, was killed.

The headline read, "Johnstone Loses Gamble with Death." He had been trying a stunt called the Spiral Glide, and began a circular descent, pointing more and more toward the ground, "like the swoop of a hawk." But a wing tip of his Wright Flyer crumbled, and "the horrified spectators watched the plane plunge straight toward the earth." Although he was "thrown from the seat as the nose of the plane swung downward, Johnstone caught one of the wire stays and grasped one of the wood braces of the upper wing with both hands." As the crowd below watched in horror, Johnstone, almost standing on the lower wing, desperately tried to adjust the wing surfaces so that they might catch the air and level off. For just a moment, it appeared that he might succeed, but then the aircraft turned over and plunged to the ground. Johnstone was buried in the wreckage. When his body was carried from the field, the band played ragtime music.

Arch Hoxsey was in the air when Johnstone lost control. He quickly landed, and he and Walter Brookins rushed to the site of the crash. But there was nothing either of them could do. The flyers knew the thin mountain air was a hazard. The day before he crashed, Johnstone had stated that he "would attempt no tricks because he considered it too

Library of Congress Prints and Photographs Division

After Johnstone's crash. A doctor is in the center, bent over the fallen flyer.

dangerous." But then Hoxsey flew "far over the foothills, which seemed to fire Johnstone to outdo his teammate."

One of the Stardust Twins had died. But Arch Hoxsey promised to honor his friend and to press on, to fly higher and farther than anyone else.

Airplane Safety

Flyers had yet to wear seat belts or any other form of restraint. Falling out of an airplane would be the cause of a number of deaths.

Part IV

Pushing to the Edge and Beyond

Lincoln Beachey's Flight under Niagara Falls Bridge. —(Copyright 1911, by Photo Specialty Co.)

Chapter 18

TWO GREAT LIGHTS EXTINGUISHED

On December 26, 1910, in front of seventy-five thousand spectators at the second Los Angeles air meet, Arch Hoxsey kept his promise to Ralph Johnstone. He reclaimed the altitude record that had recently been broken by Georges Legagneux in France. Legagneux had flown to 10,499 feet in the air, the first man to break the 10,000-foot barrier. But Hoxsey soared to 11,474 feet, almost tripling what Paulhan had done at Dominguez Field only one year earlier. He flew against a forty-mile-per-hour wind, far stronger than what most aviators would chance. After Hoxsey landed, the other flyers carried him on their shoulders in front of the grandstand.

Controlling an airplane at ten thousand feet off the ground in a totally open frame, with a strong wind rushing head-on, making it almost impossible to hear or even to turn your head, demands almost unimaginable skill. When asked, "Was it windy up there?" Hoxsey replied, "It blew so hard that my machine hardly moved and barely held its own. It was so cold that more than once I thought my carburetor was about to freeze. I made the record because I was determined to keep on going up until I passed Legagneux's record or until the carburetor froze." Three days later, Hoxsey again topped ten thousand feet, flying over Mount Wilson and the recently completed Carnegie Solar Observatory. After the flight, an army lieutenant assigned to observe the proceedings told his superiors that a thousand biplanes could transport an army of ten thousand men over mountains as high as the Alps.

Carnegie Solar Observatory

The Mount Wilson Solar Observatory, constructed to study the sun's radiation, "transformed astrophysics" and was the brainchild of George Ellery Hale, who had built his first telescope at age fourteen. The observatory, where Hale built a sixty-inch telescope, is set on a 5,710-foot peak in the San Gabriel Mountains, which at the time was one of the best locations in America at which to obtain accurate readings of solar radiation. More recently, air pollution from Los Angeles has made the location less ideal.

But Hoxsey was fearful that the 11,474-foot mark would not be declared official, and so he ascended to 10,575 feet on December 30 to be certain that he had wiped Legagneux from the record books. The following day, to celebrate the coming of the new year, Hoxsey told reporters that he intended to set an altitude record that no one would soon approach, perhaps as high as twelve thousand feet. It would be the crowning achievement of an amazing meet for the man who had taken governors and presidents into the skies. In addition to altitude, Hoxsey had won for total duration, more than seventeen hours, and endurance, more than three hours. All three represented new records.

The anticipation at Dominguez Field was intense. To have such an important record set in the West would help establish Los Angeles as one of America's most important cities.

But as Arch Hoxsey was preparing for his record-breaking ascent, he learned that John Moisant was dead.

Moisant had been in New Orleans, preparing for the 1910 Michelin Cup. He was flying the same Blériot in which he had finished second in the Gordon Bennett. This race was much longer, however, so he installed an additional thirty-five-gallon fuel tank just forward of the motor. Although his mechanics had insisted that the new tank was safe, much of the airplane's weight would now be in the airplane's nose. More cautious than the public gave him credit for, Moisant wanted to test out the arrangement. He decided to fly from the staging area to the airfield where the four-mile course had been laid out with the forward tank only partially full.

The morning was cold, with a gusty wind whipping off Lake Pontchartrain. Even for the test flight, Moisant wore so many layers of clothing insulated with newspaper that a friend likened it to a suit of armor. Moisant couldn't bend his knees enough to get into the airplane, so his crew had to lift him.

He ascended to only a few hundred feet, flew to the field, circled it twice, descended to two hundred feet, and then turned to land with the wind behind him. (No one knows why Moisant did not land into the wind, which is the proper way to bring an airplane to earth.) Suddenly, the tail of the aircraft was forced upward by a gust of wind pushing the overweight nose down into a dive. Moisant, with no seat belt, was thrown from the cockpit "as if he had been shot from a gun." The Blériot struck the ground vertically; Moisant was tossed thirty feet. His neck was broken. He survived long enough to be placed on a flatbed railroad car, but died before he could be brought to a hospital.

When Arch Hoxsey learned of Moisant's crash, he immediately sent a telegram of condolence to Alfred. But, as after Johnstone's death, he did not alter his plans to fly. Like Moisant, he took his machine up in strong, swirling winds, although not nearly as strong as those he had flown in on his earlier record-breaking flights.

He ascended to seven thousand feet, disappeared into the clouds, and, "with a thousand field glasses" following him, suddenly reemerged in a steep descent.

"The biplane came whirring out of the clouds," an eyewitness wrote. "The crowds cheered again. In the rapid downward spiraling, they saw only what they had seen Hoxsey do before these several days, cheating them into gasps of terror only to alight in smiling safety on the ground. But, within less than six hundred feet of the ground the twenty-five-mile-an-hour wind shot forth treacherous blasts. His machine was caught helplessly in the counter currents. It tumbled over then suddenly slammed to earth."

Hoxsey was killed instantly. Walter Brookins broke down when he saw the wreckage, and the other flyers sat unable to move or speak.

Although all remaining flights were canceled for the day, most spectators remained in the grandstand, many of them sobbing.

Even in a profession in which death was always lurking, Hoxsey's crash stunned his peers. Roy Knabenshue said, "Of all the aviators on the field, he was the one we least expected to see suffer an accident. He was one of the most careful men who has ever flown; he was extremely cautious about the condition of his machine and was always testing it to make sure that it would respond. I cannot explain the accident, but it appears to have been due to the gusty wind that swept over the field. Apparently Hoxsey had come down from a calm and rushed into a wind strata about 800 feet above the earth at a terrific pace. The wind caught his machine and before he was able to combat it, the biplane turned over."

Another flyer added, "The indications from the way the aeroplane moved are that Hoxsey made a mighty effort to right himself. If he had had sixty feet more between himself and the earth he might have succeeded. The machine struck almost on its bottom. This indicates that it was being righted even while the aviator was being whirled in a series of somersaults."

Among those mourning Hoxsey's death was his former passenger Theodore Roosevelt. "I am more grieved than I can say over the tragedy that came to Hoxsey. He was courageous and a splendid type of fellow. I wanted to make the trip in the air with Hoxsey because he was an American aviator and had an American machine. I admired Hoxsey for the skill he had displayed in handling his aeroplane. I felt that it was entirely safe to trust him when I ventured into the air with him....It is important that aviation be carried on....Hoxsey gave his life as a noble sacrifice."

Moisant's and Hoxsey's deaths were front-page news across America.

Within hours of each other, America's two most prominent airmen had died. Pictures and stories about aviation's darkest day dominated the front pages. Many surmised that the two crushed bodies would mark the end of daredevil flying.

Instead, despite all that had passed, it was only the beginning.

Chapter 19

AIRCRAFT CARRIER

After Eugene Ely's flight from the *Birmingham*, the navy asked Curtiss if it was possible not only to take off from the deck of a warship but to *land* there as well. Ely was eager to try, and Curtiss saw the upcoming January 1911 San Francisco air meet as the perfect place to make the attempt. The heavy cruiser *Pennsylvania* was in San Francisco Bay and was ordered to be fitted out for an airplane.

Landing on the cruiser presented a unique set of problems. Not only would the surface where Ely touched down be moving, but some means would be needed to stop the machine on a surface only forty yards long. The airplane's momentum would have to be slowed quickly but not so suddenly that Ely was pitched out, as John Moisant had been in New Orleans. Curtiss devised a system so clever that some variation of the arrangement has been in use ever since.

"The platform was built over the quarterdeck," he wrote, "about one hundred and twenty-five feet long by thirty feet wide, with a slope toward the stern of some twelve feet. Across this runway we stretched ropes every few feet with a sandbag on each end. These ropes were raised high enough so they could catch in grab-hooks, which we placed under the main centerpiece of the aeroplane, so that catching in the ropes, the heavy sand bags attached would drag until they brought the machine to a stop. To protect the aviator and to catch him in case he should be pitched out of his seat in landing, heavy awnings were stretched on either side of the runway and at the upper end of it."

Even with this extraordinary inventiveness, Ely's flying would have to be near perfect. The platform was only four feet wider than the width of the airplane, and he would be touching down at approximately forty miles per hour. A miscalculation would mean falling off the side of the ship or, worse, plowing into the crowds of sailors and visitors who would be crowded on the deck.

The first week of the San Francisco meet was subdued. The aviators flew well but without the flair and risk that had marked Johnstone's and Hoxsey's performances. No records were set; no gasp-inducing tricks were attempted; no one tried for high altitude. Even the airfield, renamed Selfridge Field, had the feel of death about it. Still, on January 8, one hundred thousand people paid to see the likes of Brookins, Latham, and other famed aviators soar over the grounds. But both in the flying and in the crowd's reaction, there was an odd sense of quiet.

On January 18, shortly before eleven AM, Ely got into his specially designed Curtiss biplane and ascended to two thousand feet. In front of seventy-five thousand spectators, he flew across the bay and then to the warship waiting ten miles away, disappearing from the view of the crowd. The bridge, deck, and superstructure of the *Pennsylvania* were packed

Aeronautics *magazine*

Ely landing on the *Pennsylvania*. Note the sandbags to aid in stopping the plane.

with crew and more than one hundred notable guests. Standing between the captain of the *Pennsylvania* and the captain's wife was Mabel Ely.

Ely circled the ship once and then came in to land, the wind dangerously at his back, as it had been during John Moisant's fatal crash. After he cut his engines but before he had touched down, an updraft caught the airplane, threatening to cause Ely to miss the line of sandbag-anchored ropes. After only a moment, however, Ely expertly dropped the tail and set the airplane down dead center on the deck, about halfway down the platform. As the hook mounted on the underside of the airplane caught the sandbag-anchored ropes, Ely rolled to a stop. A cheer went up from sailors and civilians alike! A smiling Eugene Ely got out of the airplane to be greeted by his wife, the captain, and attending celebrities. Captain Pond invited the Elys for lunch, during which the airplane was turned around. An hour later, Ely reappeared, took his place at the controls, and completed the second successful takeoff from the deck of a ship. When he landed at Selfridge Field, army and navy personnel hoisted him on their shoulders and carried him before the adoring crowds.

The aircraft carrier was born and the era of naval aviation had begun.

Ely landing on the warship.

Chapter 20

THE BOY AERONAUT GROWS UP

Among those in San Francisco to witness Ely's achievement was Lincoln Beachey, who had just signed on with Curtiss. He was new to fixed-wing aircraft, but after watching the praise heaped on a man who was now his rival, he resolved that before the year was out, all that acclaim would be his.

When Curtiss first met Beachey, he was not impressed. After Moisant, Hoxsey, Johnstone, and Ely, Curtiss was certainly unaware that he had stumbled on quite possibly the greatest flyer who ever lived. But sometimes, as it has been said, "it's better to be lucky than good." Curtiss's business manager persuaded Curtiss to give Beachey a shot, and Curtiss reluctantly went along. Even when Beachey crashed the first two times he took a fixed-wing airplane aloft—nothing like the "Boy Aeronaut" who had displayed such skill in the undercarriage of a dirigible—Curtiss was urged to keep him on.

It was not until March 1, in Tampa, Florida, that Beachey first began to show the skill for which he would later be famous. He made a flight at night in a Curtiss biplane equipped with two headlamps on the front assembly. Then he made a second flight without the lamps, and was almost killed when he was forced to fly through the smoke of smudge fires lit to mark the airfield and his machine ran into an obstruction while landing. But Beachey walked away from the crash. He would walk away from many others.

Later in March, Curtiss set up a monthlong training school in a wealthy section of North Carolina and sent Beachey to run it. The school was very popular with Carolina society, and Beachey became a local celebrity by taking up a series of noteworthy passengers, including a visiting Japanese naval officer. Newspapers reported that "Commander Saito was enthusiastic over his experience and expressed his faith in the aeroplane for naval purposes in time of war."

In May, Beachey announced himself. Curtiss had sent him as part of an exhibition team to an event near Washington, DC. Reporters had not forgotten the man who had flown a dirigible around the Capitol five years earlier. "I guess I am about the only private individual who has ever stopped Congressional legislation," Beachey said in an interview.

Warplanes

Thirty years later, Japanese aircraft carriers would launch the warplanes that attacked Pearl Harbor and brought the United States into World War II.

Two days later, he did it again. "In a hitherto unattempted and unscheduled feat, without parallel in the history of aviation," a front-page story read, "Lincoln Beachey, one of the pluckiest little aviators which the profession has yet produced, yesterday afternoon darted away from the aviation field at the Benning race track, flew over the thickly populated section of the city, and circled the United States Capitol." The flight was made in swirling, hazardous winds, and Beachey added a number of spiral dives to a spectacular ten-mile loop around the city as thousands in the streets below stood gaping. "Five years ago I satisfied a strong desire to circle the Capitol in a dirigible," Beachey said afterward, "and since that time I always wanted to perform the same feat in an aeroplane. The Capitol loomed in the distance and I could not withstand the temptation."

Curtiss lost no time in announcing Beachey's flight. He took out large ads in Washington newspapers that read, "Buy a Curtiss Aeroplane.

Library of Congress Prints and Photographs Division

Beachey over the Capitol...again.

The kind that flew over Washington yesterday, three thousand feet above the Capitol. The Curtiss machine is without a blot on its record. It has never had a serious accident. It is the swiftest, safest, and most easily controlled machine in the world." A second advertisement appeared immediately underneath. "LEARN TO

Building Planes

In those days, not only did ordinary people buy airplanes, but also a lot of hobbyists built their own. The journals were filled with advertisements for motors, radiators, wheels, and anything else needed to build an airplane—even diagrams on how to put one together. And since there were no regulations on where one could fly, anyone who could get to an open field could try his—or her—hand at aviation.

Library of Congress Prints and Photographs Division

Beachey racing Oldfield.

The Next President

William Howard Taft succeeded Theodore Roosevelt in the White House. Unlike Teddy Roosevelt, Taft would never go aloft himself. At 350 pounds, no airplane of the period could carry his weight.

FLY. Fame and Fortunes for Aviators. Good Pilots Find Immediate Employment at Big Salaries."

During that same meet, Beachey added what would become one of the most popular events at air shows—a race between an airplane and an automobile. In the first of what would be dozens of races between them, Beachey narrowly defeated champion driver Barney Oldfield. President Taft witnessed the contest and declared it "the most exciting thing I ever saw."

After Washington, Beachey tried a number of strange and difficult stunts. In mid-May in New Haven, he dropped baseballs from three hundred feet while the Yale University catcher moved underneath, trying to snag them. The balls fell too wide for the catcher to get to them, so Beachey eventually gave up.

But Beachey did make a major improvement in the design of Curtiss airplanes—and it was completely by accident. Most biplanes of the age were built in a cross design, like the *Rheims Racer* (see the photograph on page 72). The wings formed one axis and the body another, with the rudder in the rear and an "elevator" in the front. The front elevator, which designers thought allowed an airplane to gain altitude quickly, made maneuvering more difficult, but it seemed necessary for stability and safety. That turned out to be wrong.

Another aviator described how Curtiss had found out: "Beachey was flying one day, hit the fence and broke his front controller [elevator].

Even though he didn't have front control, he flew anyhow and did some wonderful flying. So I thought there's something about this…he's got no front control.… I'll take my front control off. The mechanic said, 'No. Not unless Curtiss tells me to.' But [later] we were a day ahead for a meet and I said, 'Lou, here's my chance to take my front control off.' He said, 'All right, on one condition. I'll set the thing up the day before and you come out and fly it before the crowd gets here.' So I did and it was just like you'd been shackled all your life and suddenly you tore off your shackles. Oh, it could fly! It was just a bad mistake having those two controls because they were just fighting each other."

They called the new arrangement the "headless biplane," and it became standard for Curtiss machines. Eventually, every biplane designer abandoned the front elevator. (Monoplanes, of course, had never had one.)

Library of Congress Prints and Photographs Division

Beachey in a headless biplane.

Chapter 21

THE FALLS

In late June 1911, Lincoln Beachey suddenly announced that he would fly over Niagara Falls. No one had ever braved the falls—the winds were swirling and unpredictable and the spray could easily disable the engine, sending a flyer straight into the roiling waters below. Glenn Curtiss begged Beachey not to attempt a flight that seemed certain to end in disaster. One newspaper noted that "few had believed Mr. Beachey would attempt what seemed like almost certain death in the Niagara gorge. Before the start Mr. Beachey's companions endeavored to dissuade him from the attempt, pointing out the almost certainty of failure from the eddying air currents in the gorge and the surety of certain death that awaited him if he did fail."

Beachey was certain he could do it. He "only laughed at the effort to prevent his flight."

On June 27, one hundred fifty thousand people came to watch an aviator attempt the impossible. "It was just before six o'clock," the newspapers reported, "when Mr. Beachey, in his Curtiss biplane, rose from Ninth and Niagara streets, disregarding the lowering clouds, which every moment threatened to send down torrents of rain." He flew to about fifteen hundred feet, "rising in a rapid spiral." Every eye was on him, with the roar of the powerful falls drowning out the sound of his motor. "He circled over the plunging waters twice and then shot downward in one long, swift rush directly for Horseshoe Falls."

The *New York Times* reported, "Sweeping down from immense height in a shower of rain…Beachey…passed over Horseshoe Falls, under the steel arch bridge, on down the gorge almost to the Whirlpool Rapids, then rose…and, shaved the wooded cliff." Not content merely to overcome an obstacle thought insurmountable, Beachey added an extra touch of audacity. He slowed at the brink of the falls before plunging straight down, then skimmed along "less than fifteen feet from the tumbling water…missing the top of the gorge by only a few feet." Beachey even added tricks to what was already an astonishing exhibition. Another reporter wrote, "He carried his flight, to the very brink of the cataract, seemed to hover there an instant and then, while the onlookers fairly held their breaths, executed a succession of 'Dutch rolls,' until it seemed impossible his equilibrium could be sustained."

What stunned the crowd most was that even when the airplane was buffeted by the wind and spray, at no time did Beachey seem any less than in total control. When he landed "smiling and unconcerned" on the Canadian side, Beachey declared, "It was the most exciting trip of my life," and he announced that he would repeat the flight the next day.

There was one more interesting wrinkle. The biplane was headless, the first time anyone had attempted such a challenging exploit without

An advertisement for Bosch magnetos after Beachey's flight.
Note the huge crowd on the bridge.

a front elevator. "What makes his feat even more daring," one reporter wrote, "is the fact that Mr. Beachey flew minus the front control, common to all the Curtiss machines. This portion of his biplane was broken off a short time ago and has never been replaced."

The Niagara Falls flight solidified Lincoln Beachey's status as aviation's newest star attraction. But Beachey knew that the same honor had gone to Glenn Curtiss, Louis Paulhan, Ralph Johnstone, Arch Hoxsey, John Moisant, and Eugene Ely, among others. Aviation was moving *so* quickly, records were falling *so* regularly, that unless he could keep doing the impossible and continue to be the best flyer in America, there would soon be another aviator to take his place. To keep in the spotlight, he began to fly more spectacularly. He added spins, dives, and corkscrews to his routine, and then combined them in a manner guaranteed to leave even other flyers in awe.

And in almost every performance, he ended with the Dip of Death. In addition to being terrifying in its own right, diving straight toward the ground, intentionally or not, was the way Ralph Johnstone and Arch Hoxsey had died. Each time he did it, Beachey reminded spectators— and his competitors—that he could maintain control where even the best of the other flyers could not.

As he became more famous, with more demands from the press, he became as moody and distant in private as he was flashy and colorful in public. Flyers were a close-knit group, but Beachey kept himself apart and developed few friends among his peers. "He was a weird character," another flyer observed. "A little bit of a fellow, very short, with a pugnacious jaw, and not afraid of anything, especially people."

In early August 1911, Beachey saw an opportunity to become the nation's most famous race champion as well as its most famous stunt flyer.

The Gimbel Brothers, owners of a chain of department stores, were offering $5,000 to the winner of a race from New York to Philadelphia, as long as the winning aviator passed over the Gimbels store in each city. The race took place on August 5, one week before the opening of a huge meet in Chicago. Three flyers were scheduled to compete, all in Curtiss airplanes: Beachey, an aviator named Hugh Robinson, and Charles Hamilton. On race day, however, the winds were strong and a stormy sky loomed to the west. Hamilton, the man who would take any risk, shocked everyone by refusing to fly. He told reporters that the conditions were unsafe. But "safety" and "Charles Hamilton" were words that did not go together. It's more likely that Hamilton demanded money at the last instant and Curtiss refused to pay. Eugene Ely, who had watched his own fame buried in an avalanche of Beachey publicity, immediately volunteered to take Hamilton's place.

The original plan, as reported in newspapers, was that "the contestants in the race will carry bags filled with letters, which they propose to deliver at different towns along their route. How to drop the bags so that they will not lay somebody out is a problem for the aviators. The experiment is expected to help determine the feasibility of aeroplane letter and parcel delivery." At the last minute, however, the three flyers declined to be airborne postmen, fearing that the added requirement would slow them down and damage their chances of winning the $5,000.

Beachey took off first, leaving Governors Island in New York Harbor just after two thirty PM.

Department Store Titans

Gimbels was famously in competition with Macy's. The stores faced each other at Herald Square in New York City.

He was followed by Ely and then Robinson. The three airplanes headed north, circled the Gimbels department store at Greeley Square—which is what Herald Square was then called—and turned south. Ely's engine gave out at the halfway point but Robinson and Beachey, each making one stop to refuel, made it to the end. Many thousands watched from roads and rooftops along the route, and one hundred thousand people were jammed into downtown Philadelphia at the finish. Beachey was the winner, with a time for the 112-mile course of 2 hours, 2 minutes, 25 seconds.

Both Beachey and Robinson had flown through storm clouds and were drenched and frozen from the strong winds, but Beachey seemed unaffected. "It was my longest cross country flight," he said, "but it was

Beachey on his way to Philadelphia.

so easy that I do not see why I could not fly from here to Chicago after I get something to eat."

Beachey, however, took the train to Chicago. When he arrived four days later, he was pleased to find himself the number one attraction for the greatest gathering of aviators and airplanes ever assembled.

Chapter 22

350,000 WITNESSES

Like most Americans, Harold Fowler McCormick had become fascinated with aviation. But unlike most Americans, if Harold wanted to see an air show in his home city of Chicago, he could stage it himself. And if he wanted it to be the biggest, grandest air show the world had ever seen, he could do that, too. Harold Fowler McCormick was the youngest son of Cyrus H. McCormick Jr., chairman of the board of International Harvester and one of the richest men in America, and Harold had married Edith Rockefeller, daughter of the oil baron John D. Rockefeller, who was even wealthier than his father.

In spring 1911, Harold McCormick decided to recruit other rich midwesterners to join him in sponsoring an air show that would dwarf all that had come before it, especially the Belmont meet in New York. The very best American and international aviators would be invited to participate. The meet would be staged next to—and over—Lake Michigan.

McCormick's Wealth

International Harvester was started by Cyrus McCormick Sr., who invented a horse-drawn reaper, a machine that could cut and gather grain. We still have reapers today, but they are almost all engine driven.

The crowd was expected to be more than half a million. Harold and his friends put up $200,000 to set up the event, and another $80,000 for prize money. On top of that, Harold's group intended to pay generous appearance fees, pick up the expenses for overseas flyers, and provide seating, bathroom facilities, and food and drink for spectators. Before a single flyer had agreed to appear, Harold McCormick and his associates had smashed all records for funding an air meet.

But it was going to be worth it. Attendance from the first day to the last was everything Harold and his partners could have hoped for. Newspaper photographs showed visitors literally jammed along the lakefront, hundreds of thousands at a time. On opening day, twenty-five airplanes flew over downtown Chicago, as many as ten at once. That day, a new flyer for the Wright exhibition team, Art Welsh, set a new record by flying more than two hours with a passenger. Another Wright team member, Howard Gill, won the day's honors for highest altitude, reaching 4,590 feet.

The second and third days of the meet featured thrills almost by the minute. An avalanche of spectators witnessed flying that sometimes began at two thirty AM and did not end until seven thirty in the evening. Airplanes, as many as a dozen at once, dipped and dived and swooped and corkscrewed. The *Chicago Tribune* reported, "Hundreds of thousands of people dammed the usually swift current in Michigan Avenue yesterday. The vertical sides on the west were banked as high as the highest

Aircraft *magazine*

A small section of the crowd at the lakefront.

cornice with solid masses of humanity as intent as the awed throng below in following the aviators circling in the air." Unless they arrived early, Chicagoans who had purchased tickets, a small percentage of the total, found it difficult if not impossible to reach their seats in the grandstand.

Lincoln Beachey, called "the fancy diver" in the newspapers, won a tight twenty-mile biplane race, barely beating Earle Ovington—who just weeks later would make America's first official airmail flight—with a local boy, Jimmie Ward, finishing a close third. Local newspapers declared the race "the greatest ever witnessed over an aviation course." Another Wright aviator remained in the air so long, two and a half hours, that he received a relieved cheer when he finally landed at dusk.

The First Airmail Delivery

Ovington's flight was not entirely successful. He carried a sack of mail from Garden City, New York, to nearby Mineola, but instead of landing first, he heaved it over the side of his airplane from five hundred feet up. The bag split apart when it hit the ground and the letters and postcards inside flew everywhere. An exact replica of the Blériot XI that made the flight is now on display at MacArthur Airport in Ronkonkoma, New York.

What made the meet even more unique was that with more planes in the air than had ever been seen in America at one time and aviators trying desperately to outdo one another, the event had not had a single accident or mishap.

That all changed on day four.

William R. "Billy" Badger, a wealthy amateur from Pittsburgh, had decided to fly in the meet, even though he had learned to fly only weeks before at Thomas Baldwin's flight school. Chicago would be the first time he had flown in an exhibition. Badger arrived determined to garner the same acclaim as had Lincoln Beachey. For three days, he executed dives and spirals, and basked in the crowd's applause. But late in the afternoon of August 15, he took his airplane to five hundred feet and turned it straight to the ground. At fifty feet, he tried to pull out of the dive "when his machine crumpled like a pigeon shot while on the wing." Badger was caught under his wrecked airplane. He died a short time later. He was the first aviator killed trying to copy Beachey's "Dip." There would be many more.

Two hours later, St. Croix Johnstone took a Moisant monoplane out over the lake and, a mile from shore, started a corkscrew dive. But at about eight hundred feet, "his spidery monoplane tipped a bit, shot downward with a sickening swoop, overturning just before it splashed in the water." One of the monoplane's wings snapped from the force of the dive. Hugh Robinson, flying a Curtiss hydroplane, set down on the lake and cruised to where Johnstone's monoplane was bobbing upside down. Only a small bit of the plane remained above water.

"When I reached the wreckage, the ripples were still on the water. Above the water the tail of the machine had been torn to bits by the fall. I worked the hydro-aeroplane into the wreckage and then scouted all around. I cut in circles, hoping that Johnstone had started swimming. I knew if I found him I could carry him until the launches came. I couldn't get sight of him, however. It was a full ten minutes before the launches and pleasure boats arrived. I was satisfied by that time that Johnstone was dead beneath the wreckage."

Robinson then took off. Spectators assumed this meant that Johnstone was safe, and a cheer went up. It died away quickly when they learned that Johnstone had not survived.

Two deaths in two hours—a horrible tragedy and a major blow to the exhibition. Afterward, Harold McCormick issued a statement: "I can't find words to express my sorrow over the death of the two men. I think,

Hydroplane

Glenn Curtiss was also the first man to develop an airplane that could land and take off on water.

however, that the committee has done all in its power to make the conditions of the events as safe as possible." Still, they tightened the rules so that "all recklessness will be eliminated from the meet." The committee also noted that the deaths were "part of the sacrifice necessary to the advancement of aviation…such events must mark the progress toward the goal of safe, practicable flying; that a postponement of further experimentation and encouragement of flying would effect nothing but delay without a reduction of the fatalities that must occur before the goal is reached." The day after Badger and Johnstone died, the crowds got bigger.

And they kept getting bigger. During the nine days of the Chicago meet, as many as 2.5 million people jammed in to watch the flyers. Many records were set and many new stars were created. One such star was Tommy Sopwith from Great Britain, the leading money winner at $14,020, who would go on to fame as an aircraft designer. Another was newly licensed Calbraith Perry Rodgers, who had been taught to fly by Orville Wright at Dayton only weeks before, but who seemed the sort of natural flyer who might well have a spectacular debut in Chicago.

Very large for a flyer, at six feet three and weighing more than two hundred pounds, Rodgers was a grandnephew of Commodore Oliver Hazard Perry, hero of the War of 1812, and great-grandson of Commodore Matthew Calbraith Perry, who had helped open Japan to American shipping in 1854. He was the perfect

Sopwith's Design

Among his creations was the Camel, a World War I fighting aircraft, later immortalized by Snoopy in Charles Schulz's famous cartoon strip, *Peanuts*.

figure to capture the imagination of the crowd. Wearing a constant confident grin, and with a cigar sticking out from one corner of his mouth, he was wealthy and fearless, and loved the spotlight. He was also deaf. He had contracted scarlet fever as a child, and had lost all hearing in one ear and almost all in the other. Where many flyers used the sound of the motor to help them judge how an airplane was performing, Rodgers was forced to rely on vibration alone.

The Wrights generally required student aviators to spend weeks learning to operate a Flyer safely, but Rodgers had demonstrated complete control of the aircraft after ninety minutes. He received his aviator's license on August 7, only days before the Chicago meet opened. Once there, Rodgers flew in every event he could. He won the grand prize for endurance and finished third in prize money, behind Sopwith and Beachey. Rodgers, like so many others in aviation, had arrived at an air show as an unknown and left as a star.

By the last day, August 20, the deaths had receded in spectators' memories and almost every one of the millions who had come agreed that the Chicago air meet was the most amazing event they had ever seen. The meet officially closed with a cannon shot, and then Tommy Sopwith flew Harold McCormick in a lazy circle over Lake Michigan and returned him to the landing field as the announced crowd of three hundred fifty thousand cheered.

But the "official" end of the meet did not mean the meet was over. Lincoln Beachey did not yet have his altitude record. Two hours later, after his incredible glide and dead-stick landing from 11,642 feet, he did.

No one was going to upstage Beachey.

More than any other record, more than the Stardust Twins or John Moisant's Statue of Liberty run or Eugene Ely's landing on the deck of a warship, Beachey's flight toward the stratosphere over Chicago gave the world a clear sense of how incredibly fast aviation would continue to progress. There seemed to be no limits, or at least no limits that anyone had yet approached. For airplanes and those who flew them, greatness only lay ahead.

The head of the Aero Club, America's foremost aviation association, wrote an article in *Aircraft* magazine in which he said that Beachey's flight for the altitude record was, "without question, one of the finest performances in the annals of aeronautic competition, and this is not saying little at a time when wonderful air feats are the order of the day." Then, in a passage that saw into the future, the man noted, "As to Beachey— believers in 'safe and sane' flying would naturally feel prejudiced against a man who would fly over the falls and down the gorge at Niagara, but the man compels one's unstinted admiration by his admirable control, and his precision and accuracy give a glimpse of what the future may have in store for all of us."

Chapter 23

FROM SEA TO SHINING SEA

I n May 1910, Glenn Curtiss had completed what was called the first "cross-country flight," by traveling from Albany, New York, to New York City, a distance of 150 miles. Even for so modest a journey, Curtiss had made two stops to refuel. In October, only five months later, newspaper publisher William Randolph Hearst decided to offer a prize of $50,000 to the first aviator who flew across the entire nation. The only condition was that the journey had to be completed in thirty days.

Many laughed at Hearst, accusing him of offering a prize he knew no one could win, just to sell more newspapers. The doubters had a point, since at the time, no airplane was even remotely up to the task of flying ocean to ocean, no matter how many stops it made. Hearst was able get a lot of publicity and still hang on to his $50,000.

After Chicago, though, just ten months later, flying across the United States did not seem ridiculous at all. During the very weeks that Beachey,

Rodgers, and the rest were flying before millions over Lake Michigan, another aviator, Harry Atwood, set a record of 1,266 miles on a twelve-day, eleven-stop journey from St. Louis to New York. The month before, Atwood had flown from Boston to Washington, DC, landing his Wright Flyer on the White House lawn.

But an Atlantic-Pacific flight would involve detailed planning, and cost a good deal of money. Airplanes had limited range, and because there was just so much that could go wrong in building such a finely engineered machine, aircraft often broke down or crashed. In order to succeed, an aviator would need not only a run of good luck but also an entire support team below him carrying fuel, spare parts, and possibly even a backup airplane. Automobiles were not advanced enough to serve

Harry Atwood landing on the White House lawn.

Library of Congress Prints and Photographs Division

reliably as support vehicles across a nation where good roads were rare (and in the West there were long stretches with no roads at all). That meant using railroads. The aviator would have to make certain he was flying over a railroad line—not always easy on cloudy or rainy days. And since no one knew how much or little progress the airplane might make, the support crew would have to travel in a private train.

Calbraith Rodgers was wealthy but not wealthy enough to pay for his own train. To help with the costs, his business manager approached the meatpacking giant Armour and Company and asked it to sponsor the trip. Armour agreed to supply the train and even to pay Rodgers for each mile he flew. In return, Rodgers agreed to use the trip to advertise the company's new grape drink, Vin Fiz, marking the first time in aviation history that airplanes were used to market a product that had nothing to do with flying. Armour needed the help. They had spent a lot of money promoting the beverage, but the public reception had not been good. "Tastes like a cross between sludge and horse slop," one reviewer wrote when the drink had first been introduced. The formula had been improved, but the company still needed as much good publicity as it could get.

Rodgers renamed his specially made Wright airplane *Vin Fiz*, and the private train was dubbed the "Vin Fiz Special." Armour had the Vin Fiz logo painted on the front and rear stabilizers, and the words on the underside of the wings. But product endorsements could not detract from the significance of flying coast to coast. As he prepared for the flight, Rodgers told a reporter, "It's important, because everything else I've done before was not important."

On September 17, the third anniversary of Tom Selfridge's death, Rodgers took off with great fanfare from Sheepshead Bay in Brooklyn and landed in Middletown, New York, for the night. While taking off the

Aeronautics magazine

Vin Fiz takes off from Sheepshead Bay.

next morning, the airplane's wing clipped a tree and Rodgers crashed. He wasn't seriously hurt, but the *Vin Fiz* was almost totally wrecked and needed to be rebuilt. Rodgers called Charlie Taylor, the mechanic who had built the Wright brothers' first motor. Taylor had moved his family to California and was planning on following them there, but he agreed to delay his trip in order to help Rodgers out. Taylor was paid a daily wage and remained with the expedition for five weeks, making repairs and adjustments.

And Charlie Taylor earned his money. On September 21, Rodgers was off again, only to crash again. And so it went. Rodgers crashed at least five times, had an engine explode twice, frequently became lost over the vast plains, survived a death spiral over the desert, and was almost electrocuted in a thunderstorm. In the train below were Rodgers's wife and his mother, who did not get along and fought continually, even when Rodgers was with them on the ground.

In late October, Rodgers reached Kansas and broke Harry Atwood's distance record, but the trip was taking a good deal longer than planned. Hearst's thirty-day limit had come and gone—Hearst would never pay out the money—but Rodgers never quit. As tales of his perseverance were reported in the newspapers, hundreds and then thousands gathered at each of his landing spots.

On November 6, Rodgers flew by Mount Wilson and landed at Pasadena. Even then, his troubles were not over. Taking off for the short hop

Aeronautics magazine

Map of Rodgers's flight.

Library of Congress Prints and Photographs Division

Rodgers lands at Pasadena.

to the Pacific Ocean, Rodgers crashed yet again and was knocked unconscious. He woke up in the hospital with a concussion. His airplane was
wrecked. By the next day, he was sitting up in bed, smoking a cigar, and
vowing to finish the journey.

Hoping to avoid pressure to pay the $50,000, Hearst offered Rodgers
a $500 cup instead of the prize money. Rodgers refused the offer, add-
ing some choice words about Hearst for reporters. "I can offer a million
dollars to the first man that is shot out of a cannon from here to New
York between today and next Christmas and be pretty sure of not having my money taken away from me," Rodgers said from his hospital bed.
"That's the way with some of these folks who put up big aviation prizes.
Bill Hearst had better sell his loving cup and put the money in his self-
advertising fund."

In early December, Cal Rodgers was released from the hospital, and a few days later taxied into the surf of the Pacific Ocean before a cheering crowd of fifty thousand at Long Beach.

Prize money or no, it was an amazing journey. In the end, Rodgers had more than doubled Atwood's distance record, flying 3,390 miles, as measured in the distance between towns. He had made sixty-eight stops in forty-nine days (measured to Pasadena) with a longest single flight of 133 miles, and a longest day's journey of 174 miles.

Vin Fiz advertising poster commemorating the Cal Rodgers flight.

Chapter 24

PEER PRESSURE

By the end of 1911, the speed with which aviation had progressed was as dazzling as the feats of flying that had pushed it forward. In little more than three years, since Wilbur Wright had brought his Flyer to France, airplanes had ventured miles into the sky instead of feet and could travel at a higher rate of speed than the fastest automobile or locomotive. But even more impressive was how an airplane could now maneuver in the air. Wilbur Wright's long, slow figure eights, which had left French observers awestruck in 1908, could now be performed by beginning flyers.

And the men and women who had been responsible for this amazing record of achievement were the exhibition flyers. In their efforts to amaze and astonish spectators—and induce them to pay to watch—these men and women continually tested the limits of every aircraft they flew. Builders raced to keep up. Seemingly by the week, airplanes had to be built stronger and safer, with more responsive controls and more reliable equipment. Wheeled landing gear had replaced the Wrights' track system, steering wheels were employed to turn instead of levers, and ailerons had almost totally replaced wing warping. Most flyers now wore seat belts or shoulder restraints. Some aviators turned to design themselves, as John Moisant had, trying to build an airplane that could hold up under the strain of a dive or a spin or a series of turns better than those used by their competitors.

But sometimes the equipment could not advance quickly enough, or a flyer would lack the skill to complete a maneuver safely. Death lurked every time an exhibition flyer left the ground.

Of all these exhibition flyers, no one had the impact even approaching that of Lincoln Beachey. He fascinated the public with his flying like no one who had gone before him. Even Charles Hamilton, whose daring was legendary, had never created the same excitement simply by climbing into an airplane. Hoxsey and Johnstone had come close, but their flying was usually only for height, speed, or distance. Rodgers was now famous for perseverance. But Beachey did *stunts*. He controlled an airplane better than anyone had dreamed possible. He tested the limits of both the flyer and the aircraft so that every flight was like none that had gone before. Watching other aviators compete was suddenly...ordinary. A Eugene Ely or even a Cal Rodgers might make headlines, but neither one could compete with Beachey for overall public acclaim.

Beachey knew how much the public adored him, so he always gave them their money's worth. October 2, 1911, was typical. Beachey drew twenty thousand people to see him fly in Dubuque, Iowa, a city whose entire population was only fifty-seven thousand. It was Dubuque's first-ever exhibition—almost no one who attended had ever seen an airplane fly before. Beachey made certain they'd remember it.

"When his plane left the ground at 4 o'clock the rain was pelting down," a local reporter wrote. "Through it, Beachey traveled to the south end of the park, then turned and followed back above the racecourse. On the turn, he made one of his famous dips so successfully that for a moment the machine appeared to be literally turning upside down. On righting, it glided along above the track 50 feet in the air to the north end of the park, there mounted to about 150 feet and then with a sudden turn, came swooping down toward the crowd. As they scattered in a panic, it glided off again 50 feet above their heads. The descent a few minutes later was made near the starting place."

Beachey wasn't done. "The second flight, a race with five motorcycles, proved the thrilling event of the meet. The plane sped around the course five times at the rate of 54 miles an hour, and came in at the finish 200 yards in the lead of the motorcycle riders. On crossing above the goal, instead of descending as the crowd had expected, Beachey took advantage of the rain and the low-hanging clouds to make an ascent above them. The plane mounted up into the air in big corkscrew spirals through the rain and straight into a cloud, out of it into another, and out again and into still another. The third disappearance lasted a full minute. Then as suddenly as it had gone, the machine came volplaning [gliding] toward the ground at a sharp angle. Within 60 feet of the earth it began to drop slowly, and as it touched the earth sped along a short distance to the place in which it was to be stored for the night."

But the public often confused daring with recklessness. What they did not see was that away from the spotlight, Beachey worked long and hard to perfect his flying—and to make certain he could perform his incredible tricks as safely as possible. For a long time, for example, a tail-spin meant almost certain death—no aviator had found a means to recover once the aircraft began spiraling toward the ground. Convinced he could solve the problem, Beachey flew his biplane to five thousand feet and then intentionally threw it into a tailspin. Trying different techniques as he spun downward, he eventually kicked his rudder hard against the spin and the plane slowly leveled out. He repeated the maneuver eleven times more to make certain it really worked. Then, rather than openly take credit for the service he had performed for other flyers—word of how to survive a tailspin spread almost instantaneously—Beachey simply included the move in his already stunning repertoire and called it, as he did in Dubuque, "the Corkscrew Twist."

Tailspinning

In a tailspin, an airplane heads toward the ground while spinning rapidly. It is difficult for the pilot to control and equally difficult for even experienced pilots to think clearly and act decisively.

Although Beachey might have helped other flyers behind the scenes, publicly he put increasing pressure on them to match his boldness. If an aviator attempted to complete a booking without a death-defying trick, both the crowds and the promoters felt cheated and the aviator risked not being paid. And, of course, these aviators were proud, competitive men and women, and the acclaim Beachey received rankled them. So "doing a Beachey" became shorthand among the exhibitionists for attempting a trick that was extremely risky. No trick was riskier than the Dip of Death. It had become Beachey's trademark maneuver.

The Dip of Death

Beachey was not the first to use "Dip of Death" to describe a stunt. He borrowed the phrase from a remarkable auto daredevil, a Frenchwoman named Mauricia de Tiers, who had performed a feat of that name at the Folies Bergère in her native country before being brought to America by the Barnum & Bailey circus. In a specially designed REO automobile, Mlle de Tiers sped down an eighty-foot incline, turned over, and leaped upside down to a ramp thirty-four feet away. She received $5,000 each time she performed what was officially called "L'Auto Bolide." Usually, that meant $60,000 a week, which, as the press pointed out, was "$10,000 more in a week than the President of the United States earns in a year."

When an airplane was in a dive, of course, the steeper the angle to the ground, the more exciting and the more dangerous was the stunt. One of the only flyers who could even approach the angle of Beachey's drop was Eugene Ely. His wife, Mabel, hated the Dip, but once he had introduced it into his routine, audiences demanded it every time.

On October 19, 1911, just two months after Beachey had set the altitude record in Chicago, Ely was flying at a racetrack at the Georgia state fair in Macon. Eight thousand people had paid to see the man famed for landing an airplane on the deck of a warship. On his second flight of the day, Ely took his airplane to three thousand feet, and as he was

A poster advertising Mauricia de Tiers's performance.

completing a circle of the field, "made a dip, seemingly to startle the thousands beneath him."

As the press reported, "The machine shot down with tremendous velocity and the crowd applauded, thinking the aviator would rise as he had many times before. But Ely seemed to lose his grip and the machine continued its downward plunge." Showing remarkable presence of mind, Ely actually jumped from the airplane just before it struck the ground, but the force of the fall was still too much. When officials of the fair reached him, Ely was still conscious. "I lost control," he is reported to have said. "I know I am going to die." And moments later he did.

As flyers dying at exhibitions became more common, spectators had taken to rushing to a crash site for souvenirs, sometimes fighting with one another to get them. So it was after Ely's crash, although "police fought in vain to keep them back." But still, "in a few minutes the field was cleared of every bit of wreckage. Ely's collar, tie, gloves, and cap similarly disappeared." Spectators combed through the crash site late into the night, looking for anything that had been left behind.

Mabel Ely had always been at her husband's side, at shows as well as on the road. On this occasion she was not. It was the first time since he had begun flying that she had been absent. She was on her way back to meet him after attending to business matters in New York. Mabel's mother later said, "This never would have happened if Mabel had been with him, because she never let him do anything that wasn't safe." Mabel had a different explanation for the accident—and someone specific to blame. She wrote a letter to Beachey after her husband's death. "God punish you, Lincoln Beachey. Gene would be with me now if he had not seen you fly."

In a single year, aviation had lost four of its best flyers, but the possibility of witnessing a fatal crash, there each time an airplane left the ground, only made aviation more popular. An editorial in the *San Francisco Call* read, "Ely appeared to be more than commonly skillful. He seemed to have the machine under perfect control and could alight with the utmost accuracy on whatever spot might be designated. But it gets them all sooner or later. A moment's inattention, a loose bolt or screw, a twist of wind, and there is an end."

Beachey expressed the public's fascination with danger more directly. "People come to see me die," he said.

And so Beachey continued to tempt death across America and in the process became perhaps the most famous man in the United States. He regularly earned more in a day than most Americans made in a year.

But any champion attracts challengers.

In January 1912, before he had ever flown as a professional, a wealthy Yale graduate named Rutherford Page was being billed as "the second Lincoln Beachey." Page had completed six weeks at Glenn Curtiss's aviation school in San Diego, having been trained by Curtiss himself, and had flown stunningly. He was granted his aviation license three days before the opening of the 3rd International Los Angeles Air Meet. Page announced that he would begin his exhibition career with spectacular flying.

Before adoring crowds that cheered his every move, it seemed as if Page might well live up to the hoopla. He promised that he would push Beachey to the limit and then best him in a race; when Beachey performed a series of stunts, Page swore he would "beat Beachey or break my fool neck," and then duplicated the "dips and sharp turns" in a flight "even more daring" than Beachey's. When he landed, Curtiss warned him that Beachey's maneuvers were dangerous and took years to master. Page just laughed.

Beachey was not about to lose the spotlight to a rookie. His flying, wrote one reporter, was "simply marvelous. He executed right handed and left handed spirals that were not dreamed of a year ago. With his 75 horsepower Curtiss motor and trim little machine, he left the ground and very quickly mounted high in the air. Having gained the altitude desired, he came down in small spirals that were certainly not more than three hundred feet in diameter and probably less. During these spirals he at times took his hands off the controlling wheel and even stood up."

Page decided that the best place to defeat the champion was the five-mile "free-for-all" race on January 22 that Beachey had entered. Page took his Curtiss biplane up in a stiff wind, flew out over a ravine, and then attempted to "turn on a pivot" at a treacherous spot whose constant crosscurrents led aviators to call it "Death Curve."

While four thousand spectators looked on, Page's aircraft suddenly turned nose down and plunged to the ground. Upon impact, the engine broke loose and landed on the young aviator. Page died instantly. The wreckage was burned on the spot to prevent spectators from rushing the fallen airplane to fight for souvenirs.

Page's death quickly passed from public awareness. They thirsted for a new thrill, and on January 28, Beachey gave it to them. He made a stunning announcement. A "new girl aviator, Miss Florence Walker of Seattle," whom Beachey had trained, would fly at the meet and do as well as any man.

In the early afternoon, Miss Walker, short and solidly built, dressed in a long skirt and opera cape, appeared as promised and

WEALTHY AVIATOR JUMPS TO DEATH FROM BIPLANE IN VIEW OF THOUSANDS

STARVING PEOPLE FALL DOWN AND DIE

Library of Congress: Chronicling America

took her seat in Beachey's Curtiss biplane. Then, "with broken silk garters flying and a 35 mile gale playing havoc with the draperies," the woman "performed today what probably were the greatest aviation feats ever seen on Dominguez Field." She "ascended to a great height, tilted the machine almost perpendicular, and dived back to the windswept course. The only mishap was when the wind blew off a silk garter." Then Miss Walker sent her craft around Death Curve "at 60 miles an hour, and not more than 25 feet from the ground." When the plane landed, "Florence Walker" removed her hat and wig to reveal the familiar form of Lincoln Beachey. The thousands of onlookers cheered wildly.

When the meet closed, press reports declared it "a howling success, a veritable circus in the air."

Chapter 25

DISASTER

Rutherford Page, for his inexperience, might have been forgiven for underestimating the risks of going aloft, but success had caused even some veteran aviators to minimize the dangers of exhibition flying.

In March 1912, Cal Rodgers returned to Long Beach, California, where local citizens were planning to erect a monument to honor his cross-country flight. For two weeks, Rodgers performed exhibitions, often taking passengers aloft over the Pacific Ocean. His great achievement seemed to have changed him. Rodgers had become known for his reckless flying, even ignoring friends who urged him to be more cautious. "The air is nothing to me now," he said to reporters. "I've conquered it. I have never been afraid when I go up."

On April 3, before a crowd estimated at seven thousand, Rodgers took off, "circling through the air over the city, performing thrilling manoeuvres." He engaged in a series of "Texas Tommy" figures, aerial gyrations that had gotten their name from a wild dance begun at a cabaret in San Francisco in 1910. At one point, "seeing a flock of seagulls disporting themselves among a great swarm of sardines just over the breakers, Rodgers turned and dived down into them, scattering the birds in all directions." The crowd cheered. "Highly elated with the outcome of his dive," Rodgers gained altitude and headed out to

FALL KILLS AVIATOR

Noted 'Cal' Rodgers Crushed

Calbraith P. Rodgers, who crossed the continent in an airship, who was killed by a fall at Long Beach.

Exhibition Flight Fatal to Birdman Who Crossed Continent in Biplane

sea when suddenly he went into a steep descent. At first, he relaxed his hands on the controls, as if he had gone into the dive intentionally, but was then seen desperately trying to pull them back. The airplane did not respond. Cal Rodgers crashed into the surf and perished within moments. His mechanic examined the remains of the airplane and found the body of a seagull tightly wedged between the tail and the rudder. The gull had made the rudder immovable and snapped the control wire when Rodgers tried to pull out of the dive.

Just weeks later, two friends and Wright-trained flyers, Phil Parmalee and Clifford Turpin, were flying at an exhibition in Seattle. On May 30,

Turpin was coming in to land, "careening down the airfield…at 50 mph," when an "unknown man [a photographer] rushed across the track and would have been beheaded by the machine but for the quick action of the aviator." Turpin turned away from the landing strip toward the packed grandstand but could not gain enough altitude to clear the crowd. He cut his engines, trying to bring down the airplane short of the spectators but crashed into the lower tier of boxes, killing two spectators, one of them a ten-year-old boy, and injuring fifteen more.

Although everyone assured him that the photographer was at fault and that the accident was unavoidable, Turpin was distraught. Yet when someone suggested they cancel the tour, he and Parmalee refused. They moved on to Yakima, Washington, where two days later in high wind, Parmalee took his seat at the controls. With Turpin's accident so fresh,

Library of Congress: Chronicling America

Photograph in the *Seattle Star*. The same photograph ran in newspapers across America.

the promoters asked him to postpone the flight until the wind died down. Parmalee was known for safe and careful flying, but "laughed at the persistent and fatal misfortune that had dogged aviators for the week." At about four hundred feet, he passed the rim of a canyon and seemed to be hit by a side gust of wind. He went into a vertical dive from which he could not pull out. His body was found by local farmers and pulled from under the wreckage.

Turpin was recovering from injuries he had suffered in his own crash, but insisted on taking charge of his friend's body. "It's the way of the game," he insisted. Just weeks before, Parmalee had become engaged to Turpin's sister, and both men were about to quit flying with their hides intact. "We'd been at it two years and a half," Turpin explained, "and that's more than most." Parmalee had recently told his fiancée that he believed his good luck in avoiding injury was about to run out. After Parmalee's death, Turpin vowed never to fly again.

But others continued to take to the skies. Julia Clark, who had been fascinated by the flying at the 1911 Chicago meet, traveled to San Diego and refused to leave until Glenn Curtiss personally taught her to fly. Clark showed sufficient skill to become the third woman to obtain an aviator's license, after which she immediately announced her intention to join an exhibition tour. Curtiss didn't think she was ready and told her to practice some more before joining the circuit. Clark wouldn't hear of it.

During her first flight at an exhibition in Springfield, Illinois, on June 17, 1912, Julia Clark flew into a tree and was killed instantly. She was the first American woman to die in a crash, and aviation's 146th fatality. In the 1,390 days since Thomas Selfridge had been killed at Fort Myer, an aviator had died roughly once every ten days.

None of them, however, not even Cal Rodgers, had the charisma of Harriet Quimby.

Quimby had become every bit the star in the air that she had aspired to be onstage. She had flown in exhibitions in the United States and Mexico, flown at night in front of fifteen thousand spectators at Staten Island, New York—"It was a great temptation not to keep right on flying until I got to [Manhattan]," she told reporters—and had designed a one-piece, purple, hooded flying suit that "by an ingenious device can be converted into a traditional walking skirt." Quimby had also taken up motorcar driving and was known to race other drivers through Central Park in New York.

Harriet Quimby turned out to be the ideal combination of brains, beauty, and ambition that a star needed. She always had a good quote for reporters, and made her adventures all the more popular by continuing to write articles about her exploits. Early in 1912, Quimby hatched a plan to make herself even more famous. She secretly met with Louis Blériot's New York representative and, shortly afterward, booked passage under an assumed name and sailed for England.

There, registering at her hotel as Miss Craig, Quimby met Blériot personally and they worked out the details of their scheme. If it worked, Blériot would gain a lot of publicity for his airplanes and Quimby would place herself forever in the history books.

Harriet Quimby, in a Blériot XI, planned to be the first woman to fly across the English Channel. And she would do it from England to France, far more difficult, since it involved flying into the wind for the entire trip. Quimby had traveled under an alias because she feared that if anyone suspected what she was about to attempt, another woman might make the flight first.

Women Aviators

Harriet Quimby was an inspiration to other women who wanted to take to the air. Amelia Earhart wrote of Quimby in 1932, "Without any of the modern instruments, in a plane which was hardly more than a winged skeleton with a motor, and one, furthermore, with which she was totally unfamiliar, to cross the Channel in 1912 required more bravery and skill than to cross the Atlantic today. Always we must remember that, in thinking of America's first great woman flier's accomplishments." In 1991, Harriet Quimby was one of five female aviators chosen for United States postage stamps.

At five thirty AM on April 16, 1912, Harriet Quimby climbed into her fifty-horsepower Blériot at Dover. It was a borrowed airplane—the craft in which she intended to make the flight had been damaged. A dense fog lay over the water. Within minutes of taking off, Quimby and her airplane disappeared into the mist.

In an article for *Leslie's Illustrated Weekly*, Quimby described what happened next. "I was up fifteen hundred feet within thirty seconds.... In an instant, I was beyond the cliffs and over the channel....Then the thickening fog obscured my view. Calais was out of sight. I could not see ahead of me at all, nor could I see the water below.

"My hands were covered with long, Scotch woolen gloves, which gave me good protection from the cold...but the machine was wet and my face was so covered in dampness that I had to push my goggles up on my forehead…I was traveling at over a mile a minute. I knew that land must be in sight if I could only get below the fog and see it. So I dropped from an altitude of about two thousand feet until I was half that height. The sunlight struck upon my face and my eyes lit upon the white and sandy shores of France."

Because of the fog, Quimby had totally missed Calais. She flew two circles over Boulogne-sur-Mer, and then landed on the beach at the tiny fishing village of Hardelot. "Then I jumped from my machine and was alone on the shore. But it was only for a few moments. A crowd of fishermen—men, women, and children, each carrying a pail of sand worms—came rushing from all directions toward me."

Soon, most of the town had come to the spot where Harriet Quimby had made history. Some of the men and women hoisted her on their shoulders, and a photograph was taken to immortalize the event. It was later published in American and European newspapers.

But Harriet Quimby's great triumph was not featured in newspapers to the extent it might have been. Two days earlier, on April 14—the original date for the flight—a huge ocean liner struck an iceberg in the North Atlantic just before midnight, and sank three hours later. The RMS *Titanic* took approximately fifteen hundred passengers and crew down with her.

Quimby's achievement was not ignored, however. After she returned to the United States, Armour and Company wasted little time in signing her up to replace Cal Rodgers as the face of Vin Fiz. The logo for the drink was changed from a bunch of grapes to an attractive young woman in a purple flying suit and goggles.

Six weeks later, on July 1, 1912, in a new seventy-horsepower Blériot monoplane painted "pure white," Quimby was a featured attraction at

Harriet Quimby carried on the shoulders of the residents of Hardelot.

the Boston meet. After circling the lighthouse with a passenger at seven thousand feet, she flew past the field at approximately eighty miles per hour, and then circled back to land a quarter mile farther on. For reasons that have remained a mystery, at fifteen hundred feet, her airplane suddenly pitched violently forward. First her passenger and then Quimby were ejected. Five thousand spectators watched the two turn over and over before landing in the shallows. Both bodies were described as "terribly crushed." Then, even more strangely, the Blériot regained its flight line and, "gliding off gracefully into the wind," settled into the water, where it was recovered substantially undamaged.

After the crash, there was some question as to whether Quimby and her passenger had been belted in. Another aviator claimed there had been no restraints in Quimby's Blériot. "If they had been strapped in, the accident would not have happened," he said. But others claimed that she had buckled a broad strap across a space less than a foot in front of her, and from behind and on either side, hollow tubing ran to a vertical mast on the fuselage to which support wires fastened. "How Miss Quimby could have been thrown from her seat without herself unbuckling the strap is a mystery, especially since the tubing converged to a point directly in front."

Blanche Stuart Scott, another aviatrix who would garner great fame, had been circling the harbor at five hundred feet and witnessed the fall. Although devastated at the death of a friend and fellow pilot, when asked if Quimby's death would cause her to reconsider flying, Scott replied, "Certainly not."

An Undiscovered Pioneer

For eighty years, it was believed that the first licensed African American flyer was James Herman Banning, who received a United States aviator's license, number 1,324, in 1924 or 1925. (Bessie Coleman, of mixed African American and Native American descent, had earned an international license in France in 1921.) But while rummaging through her attic in 2004, Mary Groce noticed a piece of stationery with the letterhead "Emory C. Malick, Licensee: Pilot No. 105." Emory Malick was her great-uncle, but neither Mary nor any other family member realized he had been a flyer. After a good deal of

research, Mary discovered that her great-uncle had built
his own glider in Pennsylvania in 1910 and then traveled
to San Diego, California, to enter Glenn Curtiss's flight
school. He completed his training in March 1912 and
successfully flew to obtain just the 105th license to fly
in the United States. Emory Malick went on to a career
in commercial aviation, flying for a messenger service
and an aerial photography business, and even with
passengers.

Courtesy of the Glenn H. Curtiss Museum, Hammondsport, NY

Emory Malick.

Chapter 26

THE MASTER BIRDMAN IS GROUNDED

In May 1913, Lincoln Beachey stunned the aviation world when he declared that he would never fly again. He made the formal announcement in an address to the Olympic Club in his hometown of San Francisco.

"You could not make me enter an aeroplane at the point of a revolver," he is reported to have said. "I am done. They call me the Master Birdman, but there was just one thing which drew crowds to my exhibitions—a morbid desire to see something happen. They all predicted that I would be killed and none wanted to miss the sight." Beachey then read off the names of twenty-four flyers who had been killed and said, "Those boys were like brothers to me." His recitation of Mabel Ely's letter left out her denunciation and simply read, "Eugene would be with me now if he had never seen you fly."

But Beachey's real reasons for quitting are not clear. Newspapers had come to call him "the Pacemaker for Death," but most of those he mentioned as close friends were men he either rarely spoke to or hardly knew. He had always been known for holding himself apart from other flyers. In fact, the only thing his fellows could be certain about was that they never knew Beachey well.

He didn't say what he intended to do on the ground. There was some talk of real estate, but that was probably just rumor. Whatever he did, the question everyone who knew him asked was, "How could a man who had lived with both incredible fame and incredible danger suddenly give up both?"

Beachey gave no answers. Within weeks, his retirement speech had lengthened into a newspaper feature article under his byline but was probably actually written by the publicist whom he kept on constant call.

He insisted in the article that he had no fear for himself, only for others. "In Chicago, the mother of Horace Kearney begged me not to teach him any more of my tricks. Three months later he was dead. Charlie Walsh's wife pleaded with me to have the young flyer cut out my spirals. But he said I was jealous, and that if I did them he must also to get the big money. Two weeks later, while he was in the midst of a dead reverse spiral a little wire snapped and he was dead when they picked him up. So it was with John Frisbie, Rutherford Page, Phil Parmalee, Billy Badger, Eugene Ely, Cal Rodgers, and Cromwell Dixon, all fine boys. Death has left me alone because I was a good servant to him."

Much of this is exaggerated or simply untrue. Many of those Beachey listed as dying trying to copy him were either victims of accidents or died by other causes. Cal Rodgers died from striking a seagull, which Beachey could hardly have had anything to do with. But Beachey was correct that he had set the tone of exhibition flying. He was without question the

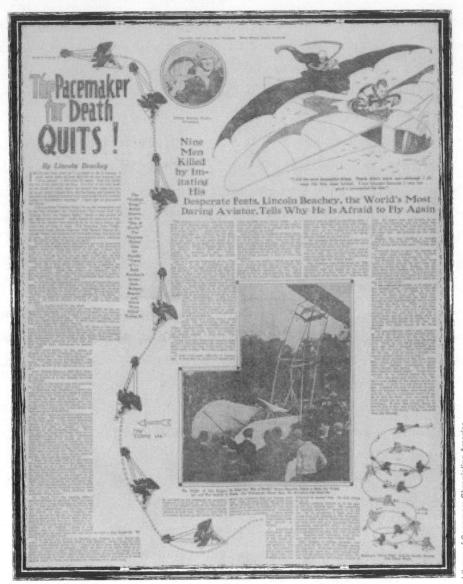

Beachey's article, printed in newspapers across America.

most reckless and the most popular of the daredevils, and his departure cast a cloud over the sport. With Beachey gone, other flyers soon found themselves booked into smaller events for less money.

Beachey drifted for a bit, making public appearances and helping at charity events. Eventually, he found his way into vaudeville. He began as a headliner, playing at important theaters, such as Proctor's Fifth Avenue in New York. There he would "entertain with views of his many perilous flights and a talk on the profession of flying." But hearing someone talk about risking death is not the same as watching him do it, and Beachey had soon ceased to be a star attraction.

He never spoke of it, but Beachey must have found it very difficult to be reduced to a mediocrity. To make matters worse, his cherished American altitude record was surpassed in July by a previously unknown aviator named Frank Burnside, who ascended to 12,950 feet. By September, only four months after he left flying, Beachey began to grumble about life on the ground. He seemed to be searching for an excuse to get back in an airplane.

A Frenchman named Adolphe Pégoud gave him one.

Chapter 27

THE LAST GREAT TRICK

Adolphe Pégoud had joined the French army at age eighteen and stayed for six years. By the time he left in 1913, aviation had become a national obsession in his country. France had more than five times as many airplanes as the United States, and more men and women went aloft there than in any other nation in the world. In addition, in France, unlike in America, the government was very active in promoting flying. It had reason to. War with Germany was becoming more and more likely, and the Germans were also producing airplanes at a rapid pace. Both nations were aware, as the United States was not, that the airplane would play a prominent role in conflicts to come.

The first thing Pégoud did after his discharge was approach Louis Blériot and ask for work. By that time, Blériot had begun to employ people specifically to test aircraft, and this twenty-four-year-old army officer seemed to be just the kind of man he was looking for. Pégoud quickly demonstrated that Blériot's judgment had been correct.

Blériot, like every other airplane manufacturer in Europe, was trying to find the best way to use airplanes in wartime. Scouting and reconnaissance had been obvious from the beginning, but there seemed to be no reason that airplanes could not also carry weapons. "Bomb dropping" competitions, usually using small sandbags, were commonly featured at air shows, and some military flyers carried pistols on board to shoot at the enemy. But it soon became apparent that the only effective way to shoot from an aircraft would be with a gun mounted directly on the body.

Beyond additional weaponry, an airplane engaging in combat would need to maneuver more effectively, or at least more effectively than its adversary. And then there was the question of how to save pilots from certain death if their machine was disabled and headed to a crash. Almost every government knew that a good pilot was more difficult to replace than the airplane he flew in.

Pégoud solved that last problem almost immediately. In August 1913, he became the first man to parachute from an airplane in flight, jumping safely from nine hundred feet. Airplanes were so plentiful in France that no one cared that Pégoud let the pilotless craft crash and be smashed to bits.

But it was not until the following month that Adolphe Pégoud performed the most elusive feat in aviation, one that was widely thought to be impossible.

The one trick Beachey had been unable to do, that no one was able to do, was a loop. In addition to the challenges for the pilot, a loop was thought to put unbearable strain on the airplane's support structure. (Aviators no longer fell out of aircraft. By 1913, harnesses and shoulder restraints had become standard for any sort of serious flying.) Even flying

Aircraft *magazine*

**The French prepare for an air war. The man at
the gun is standing so that he can fire without hitting
the propeller.**

upside down, which would be one segment of loop flying, was not considered feasible. Experts believed that the engine would stall. And they
were equally certain no one could successfully negotiate an aerial somersault without sideslipping or loss of control.

But on September 1, 1913, Adolphe Pégoud told Louis Blériot that he intended to do just that.

Blériot, who had not been able to dissuade John Moisant from attempting his Paris-London flight, had no more success with Pégoud. "It was at the insistence of M. Pégoud that M. Blériot consented to let him try this extraordinary feat," an aviation magazine reported. "M. Blériot hesitated for a long time, not because he did not think that the monoplane would answer readily enough, and stand the test, but because he had the very natural apprehension that the pilot might lose his nerve when he was upside down. But M. Pégoud felt so sure of himself, and insisted so much that in the end M. Blériot gave way, and had the machine prepared for him."

Pégoud "climbed into the machine and rose. At the moment of his departure he was by far the calmest person present." He took the Blériot XI to three thousand feet. Three attempts to turn a loop failed. Then, on the fourth, "he turned the nose of the machine earthward. For 200 feet it fell like a stone. It then turned inward till it was flying on its back, after which it rose perpendicularly upward. Then it completed the circle by regaining its normal flying position, having accomplished an apparent impossibility."

When told of what Pégoud had done, many authorities refused to believe it. But photographers had been asked to the demonstration to provide the proof.

Pégoud, however, did not seem overly impressed by what he had done. "The aviator came again to earth absolutely self-possessed. When he alighted from the machine his first remark was 'I wished I had gone another thousand feet up. Then I could have done it twice.'" When asked, "What did it feel like?" Pégoud replied, "It was just like being in

Scientific American

Proof of Pégoud's feat in *Scientific American*.

a barber's chair upside down." The following day, before a military board of experts, Pégoud duplicated the feat.

Newspapers around the world trumpeted the achievement. "Flies Upside Down for Quarter of a Mile," the *New York Times* headline read. Just below that was, "Experts Say Pégoud's Feat Is Epoch-Making Experiment in Aeronautics."

And epoch-making it was. Pégoud's loop had demonstrated that aircraft had become a good deal more stable and solidly constructed than even many experts, like Blériot, believed they were. Pégoud had also shown that airplanes could maneuver more effectively against other aircraft than most military men had thought. Which meant they could fly faster, and with superior performance than flyers had attempted. There would need to be improvements in design, of course. While he was flying upside down, Pégoud told Blériot that the gasoline leaked drop by drop out of his fuel tank, and fell into his face. The draft from the propeller blew it all over him like a spray.

Oddly, although Pégoud had completed a circle, the distance he flew while upside down kept his flight from being declared a true "loop." He fixed that on September 21, when he took up another Blériot and flew a loop that left nothing to doubt.

A Russian Was First

What neither Pégoud, Blériot, nor anyone else in western Europe or America knew was that a Russian pilot, Pyotr Nesterov, after hearing of Pégoud's upside-down flight on September 1, flew a true loop on September 9, using a French monoplane. Nesterov was at first disciplined for his stunt by his superiors, but was later promoted and assigned to train other Russian pilots. But his fame did not last. He was killed in 1914, in the first weeks of World War I. Adolphe Pégoud also perished in that terrible war, shot down in August 1915 by a German pilot who had been his student. Afterward, German aviators flew over the French lines and dropped a wreath in Pégoud's honor.

Military men saw the loop from one angle, the public from another. To ordinary people, the loop was simply another barrier that had been smashed by those brave charioteers of the skies. To one American, however, any barrier that had been smashed by someone other than him was a dare.

Chapter 28

THE MASTER BIRDMAN RETURNS

Soon after word of Pégoud's achievement reached America, Beachey—still at Proctor's theater, but now described as a "novelty"—was asked what he thought. Beachey replied that he had no doubt he could have performed the trick had he remained in aviation. It took just days of giving similar answers before Beachey had had enough. He went off to meet with Glenn Curtiss and then announced his return to flying. He added that Curtiss had agreed to build him an aircraft strong and powerful enough to match Pégoud's achievement, a biplane with a 100-horsepower motor and only a twenty-five-foot wingspan. Such a strong motor on an airplane with a tight, compact design would enable the quick and powerful turn responses that both men agreed would be necessary.

Not willing to admit he had made an error by retiring, Beachey had to come up with a good story when asked why he decided to return.

"In a year, aviation has changed from a dangerous pursuit to a serious business. The development of the flying boat means much to the world; wonderful speed combined with comfort and safety. I believe there is work for me to do that is worth any man's doing." He did admit that "perhaps it is the competitive spirit that is helping to urge me back into the game."

Flying Boats

Curtiss had further improved airplanes that could take off from or land on water, and the press called these "flying boats." Some were being designed to be quite large and would carry five or more passengers, a number greater than any land-based airplane could manage.

Curtiss set to work, and on October 7, Beachey was ready to try out the newly designed model. The test flight was not announced, but the rumor that Beachey might loop caused a large crowd to gather at the field near Bath, New York, where the airplane had been stored. Among the spectators were two naval officers who escorted sisters Ruth and Dorothy Hildreth, the daughters of a wealthy hotel owner and president of the American Wine Growers Association. To offer them a better view, the officers helped the Hildreth girls onto the roof of a barn, where they perched on the top.

When Beachey flew over the barn, he dipped his wings to acknowledge the officers' salutes. Then he steadied his airplane, prepared to learn if he would become the first American and only the third man in the world to perform aviation's most difficult maneuver.

But Glenn Curtiss had designed a flawed aircraft. The new model, powerful though it was, turned out to be far too heavy for the maneuver

Aeronautics magazine

Beachey's *Looper*.

it had been designed for. It could not pull out of a turn quickly enough or rise or descend sharply. As Beachey flew for the second time over the barn, the airplane suddenly lost altitude, and a wing clipped the roof. By reflex, the officers twisted away, but although they tried to pull the women with them, both were swept off. Ruth Hildreth died. Her head had struck the sharp corner of an automobile parked below. Dorothy Hildreth broke an arm and a leg, and her chest was crushed. She barely survived and carried the wounds for the rest of her life.

Beachey crashed in the woods, but, incredibly, suffered only minor bruises. But he was distraught about the Hildreth sisters. He checked himself into a hospital more to deal with emotional distress than to treat physical injuries. A coroner's jury determined that the crash had not been Beachey's fault. A sudden downdraft had caught the aircraft, and its weight did not allow him to overcome it.

But Beachey again spoke of retirement. Letters from both other aviators and ordinary Americans poured in from across the nation urging him not to again give up flying.

Curtiss was also extremely upset by the accident. While no one publicly suggested he had designed a flawed aircraft, he knew he had. But that was what increased demands on aircraft meant—every enhanced design held the potential for tragedy. He set to fixing the defects in the machine, and early in November, Beachey was ready. He would perform the feat at Curtiss's flight school near San Diego, California.

But first, Beachey stopped at the Olympic Club in San Francisco, where he had officially announced his retirement in May. This time, he delivered a very different kind of speech: "I just couldn't quit. Aviation is in my blood and I had to fly again," he said. Then, for a touch of patriotism, he added, "Being an American, I also felt incumbent to fly again because of that Frenchman, Pégoud, who endeavored to steal my ideas."

Pégoud had done nothing of the sort, of course, but Beachey always performed best when he felt a competitor breathing down his neck. So at North Island near San Diego on November 18, Beachey took his redesigned Curtiss airplane to 3,500 feet and then "turned the front of his machine downward. At the 1,000-foot level, he brought the machine up with a swoop and a moment later was flying head downward. The loop was complete at the 300-foot level, but instead of continuing on an even keel, Beachey went into the vertical again, and while in that position, turned the aeroplane around twice on its own axis." He therefore became the first man to spin while flying a loop.

It was a remarkable exhibition, after which Beachey acted as casual as Pégoud had. "When Beachey landed, he was asked how he did it, and he could not tell. It was all an experiment, he said."

Chapter 29

AROUND THE WORLD

December 17, 1913, marked the tenth anniversary of the Wright brothers' flights at Kitty Hawk, and even the most optimistic observer could not have foretold how quickly the science of aeronautics would advance. With aviation now a public passion, 1914 promised to be another year of marvels. Air meets were held across America and in almost every nation in Europe. Glenn Curtiss was building the *America*, a giant flying boat for a flight across the Atlantic planned for September. But that seemed just the beginning. There were serious plans to stage a race around the world!

It took just weeks after completing his first loop on November 18, 1913, for Lincoln Beachey to indeed again become the unquestioned king of the skies. He completed two loops, then three, then four, then an amazing seven. He flew upside down so close to the ground that spectators felt that they might grab his hat. With turns tighter than any other

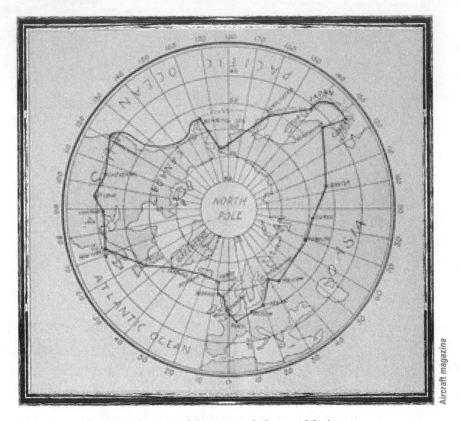

Aircraft *magazine*

Proposed route of the around-the-world air race.

aviator could master, he carved his initials, LB, in the air. On January 5, 1914, he "turned seven somersaults in a biplane," one of the loops "directly above a crowd of more than 20,000 persons." In another loop, Beachey "did what is known as the 'corkscrew twist' while his airplane was in a perpendicular position." He flew a somersault around a hydroplane.

As the most famous flyer in the world, Beachey was the man the organizers of the around-the-world race wanted the most. Beachey, however, refused to commit. But nor did he definitively refuse. His presence, he knew, would add enormous prestige to the event, but his reputation would be damaged if he fared poorly. On the other hand, if the event was a huge success and he had not participated, his standing could be equally damaged. When he was pressed by reporters in early February, he replied, "With the progress aviation has made during the past few years, anything is possible." He cited Curtiss's under-construction flying boat, *America*, as one that could cross the Atlantic Ocean. He said that he "expected to enter the race," but made no firm promise.

Three weeks later, he reversed himself and announced that he would not enter, after all. What was more, he had some harsh words for the race's promoters. "I am really sorry about schemes flaunted before the public that are on their face absurd and impossible."

As always, it was difficult to know what Beachey's real reasons were. But at the same time, he announced that from then on he would fly only machines that he designed and built himself. During those early years, many flyers—Blériot, Moisant, Sopwith, among others—had built their own airplanes, but still it took technical knowledge that not every flyer had. His aim, Beachey said, was to break all existing speed records and dominate air racing. He decided to travel to Europe to purchase motors and study the newest advances in aircraft design. In March 1914, he set sail on a luxury liner headed across the Atlantic (on the water rather than over it).

While in Europe, Beachey stayed in the finest luxury hotels, was treated like royalty by the toast of society, and basked in fame that was more widespread than he had realized. Manufacturers of airplanes and components were all desperate to have their products used by the most famous flyer in the world. In the end, he purchased two eighty-horsepower Gnome motors. He did not also purchase an airplane, since he intended to build his own. One design that interested him was the fast new Morane-Saulnier monoplane, which Roland Garros was flying with great success in exhibitions.

Beachey returned to the United States on the RMS *Lusitania* and immediately announced a cross-country tour, "promising to give a series of thrilling exhibitions such as have never been seen in this country."

The *Lusitania*

Just one year later, on May 7, 1915, the *Lusitania* would be torpedoed by a German submarine, killing 1,198 civilians, including 128 Americans. The outrage at the slaughter of unarmed civilians set the stage for the United States to enter World War I in 1917.

Library of Congress Prints and Photographs Division

RMS *Lusitania*.

Chapter 30

LOOPING ACROSS AMERICA

Beachey began thrilling Americans in San Francisco when he made the first and possibly only *indoor* airplane flight. Building had been long under way for the Panama-Pacific International Exposition in San Francisco, scheduled to open in February 1915. One of the largest buildings would be the Palace of Machinery, seven stories high, three football fields in length, and almost one football field wide. The roof of the massive structure was supported by two rows of columns running the entire thousand-foot length of the building, leaving three aisles, each seventy-five feet wide.

By May 1914, the building's shell had been completed. It was "the largest wooden frame structure in the world," with enough floor space that the entire United States Army could have stood inside. "Starting at one end, Beachey attained a terrific momentum and rose into the air to a height of fifty feet." Beachey's airplane was thirty feet wide, which left him little more than twenty feet of clearance on either side.

"He flew down the center, having to keep a straight course to prevent the aeroplane from striking the great columns of the aisle." Beachey had not asked permission to make the flight and was forced to fly through "barriers of cloth, which had been hung across the floor," giving him a "severe shaking up." When he emerged, a photographer was waiting and snapped the only known photograph of an aviator flying through a closed structure.

Library of Congress: Chronicling America

Beachey emerging from the Palace of Machinery after the first indoor flight.

"A PROPHET IS NOT WITHOUT
HONOR SAVE IN HIS OWN COUNTRY"

In consequence, not ONE-THOUSANDTH
PART has been printed or told of
AMERICA'S OWN STARTLING,
AMAZING, WONDERFUL

BEACHEY

Just back from Europe with two 80 Gnome
monocoupe (single valve) motors, ready for
engagements to

Loop-the-Loop
Fly Upside Down

To skillful, reliable aviators owning first-class
equipment, Beachy will turn over some of
the many overflow dates he has offered
but cannot fill.

All communications

LINCOLN BEACHEY, INC., Westminster Building, Chicago, Ill.

Aircraft magazine

An advertisement for Beachey's tour.

Soon afterward, Beachey announced that he would appear across the nation, often with Barney Oldfield, and placed ads in newspapers and trade magazines promoting his tour.

At one city and town after another, usually playing to crowds of twenty thousand or more, Beachey flew his own Gnome-powered biplane with BEACHEY painted across the top of the wings, easily visible to spectators when he flew upside down or in a loop. But he also introduced tricks such as the Tail Slide, in which he cut his engine and actually descended one thousand feet *backward* before starting it up and heading forward again. At Brighton Beach, in May, called the "cleverest exhibition flying New Yorkers have ever seen," Beachey "turned somersaults, dropped thousands of feet, flew upside down, and floundered about in the clear air until the spectators were dizzy." He flew inside loops, outside loops, added spirals, corkscrews, and rolls. Unlike before his retirement, he had no challengers in the air; no one thought to match Beachey's otherworldly control. For the remainder of 1914, it is quite possible that Lincoln Beachey did the finest flying the world has ever seen.

Beachey's Lost Race

Lincoln Beachey did lose a race with Barney Oldfield by two seconds. Oldfield was driving the most powerful machine on the ground or in the air, the three-hundred-horsepower "Killer" Christie. The Christie was so dangerous to drive that only a few racers could control it. Oldfield—who, like Beachey, feared nothing—loved the machine.

Wherever he was booked, reporters wrote of Beachey in such a way that local residents, many of whom had never seen an airplane fly before, could not wait to come and watch. For example, in July in Kentucky, this article appeared in all local newspapers.

> *Rain or shine, wind or calm, Lincoln Beachey, the upside-down bird man or loop-the-loop wonder, who has been engaged for one day only, Saturday, September 19, to give two exhibitions at 3 and 4:30 at the twelfth annual Kentucky State Fair, will go through the entire performance which has made him an absolutely unique figure in the world of aviation. Beachey seems to be able to successfully defy the elements and where other airmen decline to even take a chance, this intrepid aerial wonder apparently seems to revel. In fact, he claims that a calm day takes from him all joy in a flight, and*

where his compatriots loop the loop at a distance
requiring field glasses, Beachey makes his blood-
curdling whirls so close to earth that his face may
be plainly seen. He flies as easily upside-down as
he does right side up.

Almost twenty-five thousand people paid to see that performance.

A typical poster announcing a Beachey appearance.

Chapter 31

FLYING FOR THE PRESIDENT

The highlight of the tour was Beachey's promised stop in Washington, DC. With Europe now at war, he had been officially invited by Captain Mark Bristol, chief of the Bureau of Naval Aeronautics, and "was supposed to demonstrate to the lawmakers the necessity for greater appropriations for flying machines for the use of both the navy and army. It was his task to demonstrate the complete control man now had in the air."

For this exhibition, on September 28, 1914, Beachey refused to accept payment. He even spent $2,000 of his own money to bring his airplane to the capital. "I will do all in my power to bring America to the fire in things aeronautic, and to demonstrate to those who control the destinies of the nation, the advance that has been made in aero-science." Following these flights, he would offer his services to the War and Navy Departments "for any demonstration for testing purposes." He would do so "as a patriotic duty," and he "declared that under no circumstances would he accept money for such service."

Beachey had vowed to give congressmen and military officials something to talk about. And this time he would have an additional, very important, member of the audience: the president of the United States, Woodrow Wilson.

Beachey made two flights that day. He began at eleven AM near the Ellipse and headed for the Capitol. President Wilson watched from a second-floor balcony at the White House. As it had on his previous two visits, the arrival of the great aviator once again brought official business to a halt.

"When he reached the Capitol, the Senate and House office buildings were quickly emptied. Committee meetings broke up as if by magic, and Senators and Representatives, with a small army of clerks and stenographers, crowded out of the big building to take up positions in the plaza. Beachey signaled his arrival over the dome of the Capitol by turning four back somersaults in his machine in rapid succession. Then he circled the dome thrice and darted back again down Pennsylvania Avenue. He dived for the tall tower of the Post Office Department, skimmed over it and up until, when he reached the Washington Monument, he was

DARING AVIATOR GIVES WASHINGTON A SERIES OF THRILLS BY LOOPING, DIPPING AND VOLPLANING.

Around the Capitol once more.

more than 1,000 feet aloft. After alighting in Potomac Park, the aviator readjusted some parts of his engine and went up again after a wait of 20 minutes. The President again watched him as he executed fancy figures against the blue sky. The airman cut figure '8's,' dived, twisted his machine sideways, and flopped over backward many times."

Beachey's visit to Washington garnered front-page headlines, along with news of the great battles in France in the opening months of what would be called "the Great War." In the *Washington Times*, under "Breast to Breast, Millions Struggle as Great Battle of the Aisne Nears End," was the banner, "Beachey's Daring Thrills Capital," and later, "Gives Washington a Remarkable Exhibition of Death Defying Feats."

The article was a match for the headline. "Looping the loop and doing other death-defying feats high in the air, Beachey gave Washington, officials and citizens, such an exhibition of aviation as had never been witnessed in the National Capital. His closing performance, during which he cut off his power while the biplane was at an estimated height of 2,500 feet, looped the loop and, righting himself after vol-planing fully 1,000 feet upside down, landed lightly as a wind-blown leaf, was

The Battle of the Aisne

This headline-grabbing battle occurred after French forces stopped a German attack just outside Paris in August 1914. The Germans had advanced rapidly, but French reinforcements were brought up, many in Paris taxicabs, and both sides dug in for what would be a terrible four years of bloodshed. The battle line would be just outside Reims, where, only five years earlier, Glenn Curtiss had helped usher in the age of exhibition flying.

Beachey sharing headlines with the Great War.

the climax of a performance such as Washington residents have read of, but never have seen."

Beachey's flying caused such a stir that at one point an ambulance was dispatched from the Emergency Hospital, "loaded with interns, to make a wild dash to the polo field in Potomac Park, where, according to a hurried call telephoned to the hospital, the aviator had fallen from a considerable height. When the ambulance surgeons reached the polo field, Beachey was talking with his mechanicians and others, the biplane was being tinkered over in preparation for another flight, and the ambulance corps found the run had been made for nothing."

Tens of thousands had stood in the streets, in parks, and on roof-tops to watch Lincoln Beachey fly. Afterward, he said his exhibition was "my contribution to the cause of aviation. I hope my flight will result in the members of Congress realizing that aviation is not to be regarded lightly, and also that we have in America as good aeroplanes and pilots as there are in Europe." Reporters observed that congressmen, "from their exclamations of awe and wonder at his flight and their congratulations following it, [felt] he succeeded perfectly."

President's Wilson's reaction, however, was not what Beachey had hoped for. The president watched the aviator "turn a double aerial som-ersault over the White House grounds some 1,600 feet up in the air, then drive his tiny aeroplane through hair-raising revolutions." Wilson "heaved a sigh of relief when the machine darted off in a straight line toward the Capitol at the other end of Pennsylvania Avenue."

But when he was asked what he thought of the exhibition, President Wilson said only, "Wonderful, but startlingly reckless." President Wil-son was in the minority. For most Americans, Beachey's maneuvers had only added to the fascination with airplanes. For military men, it was a glimpse of what could be a new and startling weapon of modern warfare.

Chapter 32

MONOPLANE

The Panama-Pacific International Exposition began on February 20, 1915. At noon, after "a series of artillery salutes from the army posts on San Francisco Bay," President Wilson pressed a button in the East Room of the White House in Washington, DC, which went to an electric switch that sent a "spark through the air from Washington to be received on the radio antenna hung on the exposition's Tower of Jewels." That "caused the doors of the exhibit palaces to open and the machinery in machinery hall to start."

Just the idea that electricity could be controlled from across the nation signaled how unique, modern, and spectacular the Panama-Pacific would be. The fair had been publicized for months, and millions planned to visit the wonders. Just after President Wilson threw the switch, Beachey flew over the midway, causing the entire throng of opening-day visitors to crane their necks to watch.

Library of Congress: Chronicling America

Spectators watching Beachey fly over the fairgrounds.

With all the stunning exhibits—the submarine, the Ford automobiles, the Liberty Bell, the replicas of natural wonders—airplanes were the number one attraction, and Lincoln Beachey remained the exposition's star.

Four days after the opening, he performed his thousandth loop, as well as "two entirely new and death defying stunts," while his mother watched from 435 feet up, at the top of the Tower of Jewels. She "cried out only once," when Beachey wrote "1000" from a mile up in the sky. Days later, he once again flew an incredible seven loops, more than any other aviator could manage.

On days Beachey went into the sky, the crowds swelled. His flying was so amazing, it became almost impossible for him to outdo himself. It was on March 14 that he decided to try. He announced that for the very first time he would perform his most famous stunt, the Dip of Death, in a monoplane.

Beachey during a seven-loop run at the Panama-Pacific Exposition.

Beachey had used the Morane-Saulnier design, powered with an eighty-horsepower Gnome motor that would make his airplane very, very fast. "My brother wanted speed," Hillery Beachey said later. "That's the main thing. The first thing he did with his new monoplane was to fly it over the ocean beach. He'd marked off a mile there with the speedometer in his car. He timed himself over that and he did 110 miles per hour."

To make the machine light and strong, Beachey had used aluminum in the body and wings. The wings were braced by a series of support wires, instead of struts, from the top and bottom of the body to the wing surface.

Lincoln Beachey made three flights that March 14. The first ended quickly when he had to land to retune the engine. In the second, according to *Aeronautics* magazine, "he shot straight up into the air, climbing to about 5,000 feet before leveling off. He made a trip over San Francisco, then turned around and crossed the bay to Sausalito, after which he made three or four excellent loops, and glided down the grounds at a slow angle and landed safely. The monoplane was a beautiful sight in the air, having graceful lines, and very fast."

After he landed, Beachey taxied the monoplane out of sight of the crowd to check it one more time before taking it up to do what no one had ever done before.

Thirty minutes later, Lincoln Beachey rolled his monoplane out before the assembled throng, acknowledged the spectators with a short wave, and then took off. He headed out over the harbor, where many naval vessels were anchored. Thousands of sailors added to his audience.

An observer on the scene wrote, "Beachey went up approximately 4,000 feet, made several loops, and then circled up until he had gained approximately 5,000 or 6,000 feet altitude, made another loop and then started for the ground perpendicularly."

As soon as his brother had begun to taxi from the staging area, Hillery Beachey boarded a small boat that took him to one of the naval ships. He stood on the deck and watched his brother enter the dive. He said later that he would be relieved when this routine was over. He had designed airplanes himself and he just wasn't certain about this one. But he trusted his brother—Beachey had told Hillery he would take no chances. Hillery thought back to the time in Dallas when his brother had done the Dip twice, each time pulling out when only fifteen feet from the ground, landing the second time only a foot from where he'd set down the first. This time, he would pull out of the dive high up, five hundred feet, just in case the controls did not respond as they did on a biplane.

Not taking his eyes from the monoplane, Hillery exhaled when he saw that the dive was perfect. But then, just when Beachey started to level out and Hillery thought the worst was over, the unthinkable happened.

Hillery heard a crack, "like the breaking of a ship's mast." One wing then "folded straight back and exploded like a prefire of the motor. It was not long before the other did the same thing." Hillery stood horrified as his brother, helpless to save himself, plunged into San Francisco Bay, not twenty yards from where he was standing.

"Thousands of spectators rushed to the nearby waterfront," a reporter wrote, "but with the exception of a few splintered fragments of the aeroplane floating on the surface of the water, no sign of the wrecked aircraft could be seen." Boats were immediately sent to the crash site and divers, who had been stationed for just such an emergency, dived into the water.

But it was no use. The water was murky and it took two hours to locate the wrecked monoplane. It was later determined that the speed of the aircraft and the aluminum construction had contributed to the failure of the wings to withstand the pressure of Beachey's attempt to pull out of the dive.

But it was only after the wreckage had been raised to the surface that the most bizarre fact came to light. Although he had hit the water at high speed, Lincoln Beachey did not die from the impact. He had not even lost consciousness. His leg had been broken in the crash but he was otherwise unhurt. As he sank into forty feet of water, he clawed desperately at his harness and the tangle of cables and metal, trying to free himself from the wreckage so that he could float to the surface.

But he could not. In the end, the greatest aviator America has ever seen died of drowning.

Epilogue

TURNING THE PAGE

The death of Lincoln Beachey marked the end of the exhibition era. The years of daredevil flying had brought untold thrills to millions—and cost the lives of hundreds of brave men and women. But in giving their lives, they contributed to the advancement of controlled, powered flight in ways that would have seemed unimaginable just a decade before. In December 1903, Orville Wright had flown a distance of 852 feet about 20 feet off the ground at approximately twelve miles per hour; at the time of Lincoln Beachey's death, aviators were regularly flying more than one hundred miles without refueling, attaining altitudes higher than twelve thousand feet, and reaching speeds greater than one hundred miles per hour. The list of improvements to airplanes during the same period would fill pages: ailerons, steering wheels, seat and shoulder restraints, wheeled landing gear, removal of the front elevator, floats for landing on and taking off from water, rotary and V motors, instruments, metal frames.... Everything was different. By 1915, not one single feature of the original Wright Flyer remained in use.

Flying would advance still more in coming years. World War I raged in Europe and in 1917 drew in the United States. The bloody conflict would (as war always does) propel forward any technology that may be of use either in killing the enemy or protecting against being killed by them. Airplanes were a glamorous addition to combat and spawned an entire new generation of aviators.

Today, we have airplanes that can fly hundreds of people thousands of miles while offering them food, movies, television, and even Internet service. Major airports may track hundreds of flights on their radar at any one time. Air travel has become so common that most Americans, and many people around the world, have been passengers on an airplane, often while still children.

But the debt we owe to those early exhibition flyers is undiminished— to Cal Rodgers, Harriet Quimby, Eugene Ely, John Moisant, Ralph Johnstone, Arch Hoxsey, Adolphe Pégoud, Roland Garros, and of course Lincoln Beachey, and many, many others. Most of these men and women are forgotten now, but they were heroes. For it is people like these who do what most cannot—expand the boundaries of human experience so that the rest of us may enjoy a richer and fuller life.

TIME LINE

1799: George Cayley produces a medallion, with the design on the front for a glider, and on the back, an illustration of the four forces that figure in flight: lift, drag, gravity, and thrust.

May 1896: Samuel Pierpont Langley, secretary of the Smithsonian Institution, flies a powered, unmanned machine, which he called an "aerodrome," over the Potomac River. His friend, Alexander Graham Bell, watches the demonstration.

May 1899: Wilbur Wright sends a letter to the Smithsonian Institution asking for any materials they have available on flight.

September 1900: The Wright brothers make their first trip to Kitty Hawk, North Carolina.

1891: Otto Lilienthal begins his glider flights. Over the next five years he would make more than two thousand such runs.

1891: Civil engineer Octave Chanute, famed for designing bridges and the Chicago stockyards, begins to study the "flying problem." In 1894, he publishes *Progress in Flying Machines*, a book that will be read by almost everyone seeking to achieve powered flight. He will correspond with would-be aviators all over the world and provide information and sometimes funding to help them. Among those whom he helps is Wilbur Wright.

1898: Edson Gallaudet, an instructor at Yale, flies an unmanned glider using the control system Wilbur Wright would later call "wing warping." Fellow faculty members discourage him from continuing his research.

August 1901: Gustave Whitehead (it has been claimed) flies a fixed-wing aircraft at Bridgeport, Connecticut.

October and December 1903: Langley's two attempts to adapt his aerodrome to manned flight fail spectacularly.

December 17, 1903: The Wright brothers make their historic flights at Kitty Hawk. They do not announce their triumph but instead return home to perfect their airplane for commerical development. They will not fly again publicly for another four years.

May 22, 1906: The Wright brothers receive their patent.

June 14, 1906: Lincoln Beachey sails an airship around the Capitol in Washington, DC.

September 1906: Alberto Santos-Dumont flies his *14bis* in Paris, France.

July 4, 1908: Glenn Curtiss flies his airplane *June Bug* more than a mile to win a prize offered by *Scientific American*.

August 8, 1908: Wilbur Wright brilliantly demonstrates his airplane in France.

September 17, 1908: Orville Wright is flying with equal brilliance in the United States, near Arlington, Virginia, when a freak crash injures him terribly and kills Thomas Selfridge.

October 1904: Thomas Scott Baldwin brings the *California Arrow* to the Louisiana Purchase Exposition in St. Louis, and the dirigible airship is born.

January 24, 1907: Glenn Curtiss sets a land speed record of 136.36 miles per hour on a motorcycle.

September 1907: Alexander Graham Bell forms the Aerial Experiment Association at his summer home in Nova Scotia. The group includes Glenn Curtiss and a promising young army lieutenant, Thomas Selfridge.

July 25, 1909: Louis Blériot flies across the English Channel.

August 28, 1909: Glenn Curtiss wins the Gordon Bennett Cup at Reims.

September 29, 1909: At the Hudson-Fulton Celebration, Wilbur Wright makes a triumphant flight over New York Harbor with American flags streaming from the bottom of the wings of his biplane.

January 11, 1910: Louis Paulhan sets an altitude record at the First Los Angeles International Air Meet.

May 29, 1910: Glenn Curtiss flies from Albany, New York, to New York City, the first "cross-country" flight.

August 19, 1910: At an air meet in New Jersey, Ralph Johnstone and Arch Hoxsey become the first people to fly at night.

1911: Isaac Newton Lewis develops a light machine gun, which will be mounted on aircraft to create the first true fighter planes.

June 27, 1911: Lincoln Beachey flies at Niagara Falls.

August, September 1911: Harriet Quimby and Matilde Moisant become the first women to be licensed aviators.

October 30, 1910: John Moisant wins the Statue of Liberty race and becomes the most famous aviator in America.

November 14, 1910: Eugene Ely makes the first flight from the deck of a ship.

November 23, 1910: Octave Chanute dies. Everyone in aviation mourns.

December 31, 1910: John Moisant and Arch Hoxsey are killed on the same day.

August 20, 1911: Lincoln Beachey flies 11,642 feet into the sky over Lake Michigan.

December 10, 1911: Cal Rodgers reaches the Pacific Ocean to complete America's first coast-to-coast flight.

January 1912: Glenn Curtiss produces the first true hydroplane, the *Flying Fish*.

March 20, 1912: Emory Malick becomes the first licensed African-American aviator.

April 16, 1912: Harriet Quimby becomes the first woman to fly across the English Channel.

May 1913: Lincoln Beachey announces he will give up exhibition flying.

September 1, 1913: Adolphe Pégoud flies the first loop.

October 7, 1913: Lincoln Beachey comes out of retirement.

March 14, 1915: Lincoln Beachey dies in San Francisco Bay, and the exhibition era comes to an end.

May 30, 1912: Wilbur Wright dies at his home in Dayton, Ohio.

July 1, 1912: Harriet Quimby is killed in a crash in Boston Harbor.

June 1914: Elmer Sperry adapts the gyroscope for use as an automatic stabilizer on aircraft.

August 1914: World War I begins.

GLOSSARY

aerodynamics. A field of science in which the motion of air (or other gases) is studied, as well as the effects the moving air has on solids it comes in contact with, such as airplane wings.

aeronaut. The pilot of an airship, balloon, or any other lighter-than-air craft.

aileron. "Little wing"—a movable surface, mounted between the top and bottom wings of a biplane, or at the rear of the wing on a monoplane, which allows the aviator to correct roll or to bank in a turn.

airfoil. A wing, aileron, or stabilizer that helps provide lift or control for an aircraft by changing the direction of the air through which it moves.

airframe. The body of an airplane.

airplane. A heavier-than-air craft with a propulsion system (propellers, jet engines, etc.) kept aloft by lift generated when air moves over fixed wings.

airship, or dirigible. A lighter-than-air aircraft with a motor to propel it forward, which can also steer.

anhedral. An arrangement by which wings slant downward from the center of the airplane.

attitude. The position of an airplane in flight determined by its relationship to the horizon, and the angle at which its wings are dipping in one direction or another. Attitude is restored with ailerons or wing warping.

banked turn. A turn in which an airplane inclines, almost always toward the inside of the curve.

biplane. An airplane with two sets of wings, one over the other, held stable by struts and wires.

dihedral. An arrangement by which wings slant upward from the center of the airplane.

drag. A force created when air moves over the wings and fuselage and tends to slow an airplane's thrust or forward momentum.

fixed-wing aircraft. An airplane that achieves lift by air moving over wings or other surfaces that are rigidly attached to the fuselage.

fuselage. The body of the airplane, to which the wing, tail, rudder, and sometimes engines are attached.

hydroplane. An airplane that can land and take off on water.

internal combustion engine. A motor consisting of one or more cylinders containing pistons, which are fit exactly to the cylinders' shape. Power is generated when explosions inside these cylinders force down the pistons, which push a rod attached to a shaft, and thereby convert up-and-down motion to circular motion.

lift. The force that allows an airplane to ascend or remain in the air. An airplane generates lift when the air moving over the aircraft, mostly the wings, is angled upward by the curve of the wing and fuselage.

monoplane. An airplane with one set of wings extending in opposite directions from the fuselage.

rudder. A movable control panel, usually attached vertically at the rear of an airplane, that, with ailerons, is used for making turns.

strut. A solid piece connecting two surfaces and holding them in constant position.

wing warping. A means of controlling an airplane's attitude and allowing it to bank in a turn by twisting the wing tips on either side in opposite directions.

NOTES

Introduction: The Man Who Owned the Sky

4–5   **"in wide sweeps that swung him out over the city"**: Beachey's flight was described in the *Chicago Daily Tribune*, August 21, 1911, p. 1.

7   **"You are about to witness the premier birdman of them all"**: There is no specific record of what Beachey announced through the megaphone before his flight, but what is written here represents a fairly standard pitch to a crowd.

Chapter 1: The First Birdman

13   **"aroused a passive interest which had existed since my childhood"**: Wilbur Wright's pronouncements are all taken from the Wright brothers' papers, an extraordinary collection at the Library of Congress, https://www.loc.gov/collections/wilbur-and-orville-wright-papers.

Chapter 2: Parachutes and Gasbags

14–21   **"a man is equally at home on wire, rope or ground"**: Thomas S. Baldwin, "The High Seas of Space," *National Magazine* 28, no. 4 (April–September 1908), pp. 457–60. Baldwin's autobiographical article seems, by his standards, reasonably accurate.

20   **"like pushing a candle through a brick wall"**: *Engineering Magazine*, December 14, 1906, p. 792.

20–21   **"chanced to see a new motorcycle, the motor of which seemed to be exactly what he wanted to propel his new airship"**: Glenn Hammond Curtiss and Augustus Post, *The Curtiss Aviation Book* (New York: Frederick A. Stokes Company, 1912), p. 29. The book was ghostwritten for Curtiss by aviation pioneer Augustus Post, who also included some sections under his own name.

As with most of the accounts of the period, liberties were often taken with specifics, but the basic facts seem generally accurate.

Chapter 3: Into the Wind

26   **"Turning, circling, wheeling this way and that…with the wind and against the wind"**: Knabenshue's flight was described in "Aeronaut at Fair Accomplishes Greatest Aerial Feat on Record," *St. Louis Republic*, November 1, 1904, p. 1.

Chapter 4: The Boy Aeronaut

30   **"Beachey navigated the huge vessel with wonderful dexterity and precision"**: "Airship Proves to Be Good Letter Carrier," *Los Angeles Herald*, September 27, 1905, p. 1, http://chroniclingamerica.loc.gov/lccn/sn85042462/1905-09-27/ed-1/seq-1/.

30–31   **"I stand on this two-inch beam along the under side of the framework"**: Beachey was written up in newspapers across the nation, many of which can be viewed online at the Library of Congress's Chronicling History website. Beachey's description of flying, for example, is from "Lincoln Beachey, Boy Aeronaut," *Spokane Press*, August 26, 1905, p. 4, http://chroniclingamerica.loc.gov/lccn/sn88085947/1905-08-26/ed-1/seq-4.

32–33   **"Soaring like a bird hundreds of feet above the earth"**: *Washington Times*, June 14, 1906, p. 1.

Chapter 6: Takeoff!

44   **"If the rear edge of the right wing tip"**: Letter from Wilbur Wright to Octave Chanute, May 13, 1900, hdl.loc.gov/loc.mss/mcc.006.

Chapter 8: Triumph…

52   **"Frenchmen seemed to vie with each other"**: "Wilbur Wright's Flights in France," *Aeronautics* 3, no. 3 (September 1908), p. 6, https://archive.org/details/aeronautics34aero.

53   **"public interest and enthusiasm continues to increase"**: This letter, from the Wright brothers' papers, was written by Wilbur to Orville on September 6, 1908, https://www.loc.gov/collections/wilbur-and-orville-wright-papers.

54   **"Over the roofs of the post buildings he sailed"**: Orville's flight was reported in newspapers across America, including the *New York Times*, September 10, 1908, p. 1.

Chapter 9: ...and Tragedy

56   **"Mr. Wright...made a wrong move and headed into a dive"**: Glenn Curtiss wrote a letter to Alexander Graham Bell, quoted in C. R. Roseberry, *Glenn Curtiss: Pioneer of Flight* (Garden City, NY: Doubleday, 1972), p. 125.

57   **"There was a crack like a pistol shot coming from above"**: W. S. Clime, "The Orville Wright Disaster," *Aeronautics* 4, no. 3 (March 1909), p. 108.

Chapter 10: Crossing the Channel

61   **"the handling of the aeroplane was simplicity itself"**: Wilbur's activities in France were widely reported in American newspapers. Count Lambert's remark is from "Wright Teaches Flying; Count de Lambert, His Pupil, Says Handling the Aeroplane Is Simple," *New York Times*, October 29, 1908, p. 4.

Chapter 11: The Week of Miracles

71–74   Curtiss's description of the Reims meet from Glenn Hammond Curtiss and Augustus Post, *The Curtiss Aviation Book* (New York: Frederick A. Stokes Company, 1912), pp. 65–66.

Chapter 12: A Week of Miracles in America

77   **"a great boost for Los Angeles, and in fact all California"**: Ferris's buildup of the air show was regularly reported in local newspapers, this one being from the *Los Angeles Herald*, November 8, 1909, p. 5.

80   **"Paulhan was cheered madly"**: The Los Angeles air meet was big news across the United States. This description of Paulhan's flying appeared in "Paulhan Flies," *New-York Tribune*, January 11, 1910, p. 1.

80   **"demonstrated beyond the question of a doubt the practicability of the aeroplane"**: The impact of the meet is from *Aeronautics* 6, no. 3 (March 1910), p. 80.

83   **"turned a somersault and fell"**: "Aviator Hamilton Severely Injured," *Arizona Republican*, March 13, 1910, p. 1, http://adnp.azlibrary.gov/cdm/ref/collection/sn84020558/id/34687.

Chapter 13: The Stardust Twins

85   **"All Hoxsey could talk about was the air meet"**: Hoxsey was described in an interview with Beckwith Havens, "Reminiscences of Beckwith Havens: Oral History, 1960," Columbia Center for Oral History, Columbia University Libraries, New York, NY, https://clio.columbia.edu/catalog/4075358.

86   **team members were forbidden to drink, smoke, or swear**: Flying for the Wrights was described in an interview with Frank T. Coffyn, "Reminiscences of Frank T. Coffyn: Oral History, 1960," Columbia Center for Oral History, Columbia University Libraries, New York, NY, https://clio.columbia.edu/catalog/4074043.

Chapter 15: The World Comes to New York

97   **"they were steadily gaining in altitude, and then began to drift backward"**: The Belmont meet in New York was widely reported in newspapers and magazines across America. The description of flying backward comes from "Knabenshue Says Dead Man Exceeded Orders," *Los Angeles Herald*, November 18, 1910, p. 3.

102   **"it was something like meeting a ghost"**: It is not known if the reporter's allusion to a "ghost" is because of Halloween. *New York Times*, October 31, 1910, p. 2.

102   **"My brother doesn't fly to land. He flies to win"**: Doris L. Rich, *The Magnificent Moisants: Champions of Early Flight* (Washington, DC: Smithsonian Institution Press, 1998), p. 69.

103   **"Moisant, his face red from the fanning of the cold air"**: This description of Moisant's reaction comes from the *New York Times*, October 31, 1910, p. 1.

Chapter 17: Flying for the Navy

111   **"a platform sloping downward, and wide enough to allow an aeroplane set up on it"**: Description of platform from Glenn Hammond Curtiss and Augustus Post, *The Curtiss Aviation Book* (New York: Frederick A. Stokes Company, 1912), pp. 116–19.

113   **"thrown from the seat as the nose of the plane swung downward"**: Johnstone's death was widely reported. "Johnstone Loses Gamble with Death," *Boston Daily Globe*, November 18, 1910, p. 1.

Chapter 18: Two Great Lights Extinguished

119–120   **"I thought my carburetor was about to freeze"**: Hoxsey's description comes from the *New York Times*, December 27, 1910, p. 4.

122–23   **"whirled in a series of somersaults"**: Description of Hoxsey's crash from the *New York World*, January 1, 1911, p. 1; and the *San Francisco Call*, January 1, 1911, p. 1.

123   **"I am more grieved than I can say"**: Theodore Roosevelt's comments were widely published, here from the *San Francisco Call*, January 2, 1911, p. 12.

Chapter 19: Aircraft Carrier

126–27 **"The platform was built over the quarterdeck"**: Curtiss's description from Glenn Hammond Curtiss and Augustus Post, *The Curtiss Aviation Book* (New York: Frederick A. Stokes Company, 1912), p. 120.

Chapter 20: The Boy Aeronaut Grows Up

131 **"Commander Saito was enthusiastic over his experience"**: "General News," *Aircraft* 2, no. 3 (May 1911), p. 86.

131–32 **"flew over the thickly populated section of the city, and circled the United States Capitol"**: Description of Beachey's flight around the Capitol from *Washington Herald*, May 6, 1911, pp. 1, 3.

134–35 **"Even though he didn't have front control, he flew anyhow"**: Interview with Beckwith Havens, "Reminiscences of Beckwith Havens: Oral History, 1960," Columbia Center for Oral History, Columbia University Libraries, New York, NY, https://clio.columbia.edu/catalog/4075358.

Chapter 21: The Falls

136 **Glenn Curtiss begged Beachey not to attempt a flight**: Attempts to dissuade Beachey and the description of his dive come from a syndicated article, given here from *Bridgeport Evening Farmer*, June 28, 1911, p. 9.

137 **"Sweeping down from immense height in a shower of rain"**: *New York Times*, June 28, 1911, p. 1.

139 **"A little bit of a fellow, very short, with a pugnacious jaw"**: Description of Beachey from interview with Beckwith Havens, "Reminiscences of Beckwith Havens: Oral History, 1960," Columbia Center for Oral History, Columbia University Libraries, New York, NY, https://clio.columbia.edu/catalog/4075358.

Chapter 22: 350,000 Witnesses

144–45 **"Hundreds of thousands of people"**: Description of the Chicago events from *Chicago Daily Tribune*, August 13, 1911, p. 1.

147 **"his spidery monoplane tipped a bit"**: The description of Johnstone's crash comes from *Aeronautics* 9, no. 3 (September 1911), p. 92.

148 **"I can't find words to express my sorrow"**: McCormick's reaction from *Chicago Daily Tribune*, August 16, 1911, p. 1.

150 **"without question, one of the finest performances"**: Article by G. F. Campbell Wood, "Impressions of the Big Meet," *Aircraft* (September 1911), p. 229.

Chapter 23: From Sea to Shining Sea

153   **"Tastes like a cross between sludge and horse slop"**: Description of Vin Fiz is widely available, for example in the *Atlantic*, March 25, 2011.

156   **"I can offer a million dollars to the first man that is shot out of a cannon"**: Rodgers's remarks about Hearst come from the *San Francisco Call*, November 9, 1911, p. 1.

Chapter 24: Peer Pressure

160   **"When his plane left the ground at 4 o'clock"**: Beachey's exploits from *Aero and Hydro*, October 7, 1911, p. 10.

163   **"The machine shot down with tremendous velocity"**: Ely's death reported in the *San Francisco Call*, October 20, 1911, p. 1.

164   **"God punish you, Lincoln Beachey"**: Mabel Ely's letter quoted in Frank Marrero, *Lincoln Beachey: The Man Who Owned the Sky* (San Francisco: Scottwall, 1997), p. 81.

164   **"Ely appeared to be more than commonly skillful"**: Editorial from *San Francisco Call*, October 20, 1911, p. 6.

165–66   **"He executed right handed and left handed spirals"** and **"a new girl aviator"**: *Aeronautics* 10, no. 2 (February 1912), p. 63, https://archive.org/details/aeronautics910aero.

166–67   **"with broken silk garters flying"**: Description of "Florence Walker," from *San Francisco Call*, January 28, 1912, p. 1.

Chapter 25: Disaster

168–69   **"circling through the air over the city"**: Description of Cal Rodgers's crash from "Fall Kills Aviator," *San Francisco Call*, April 4, 1912, p. 1.

170   **"careening down the airfield…at 50 mph"**: Description of Turpin's crash from "Find Woman's Hand under Wrecked Plane," *Berkeley Daily Gazette*, May 31, 1912, p. 1.

173–74   **"I was up fifteen hundred feet within thirty seconds"**: "An American Girl's Daring Exploit." *Leslie's Illustrated Weekly*. May 16, 1912.

175   **Blériot monoplane painted "pure white"**: "Aviatrice Killed," *San Francisco Call*, July 2, 1912, p. 5, http://chroniclingamerica.loc.gov/lccn/sn85066387/1912-07-02/ed-1/seq-5.

Chapter 27: The Last Great Trick

185   **"But M. Pégoud felt so sure of himself…that in the end M. Blériot gave way"**: Pégoud and Blériot are described in *Flight*, September 13, 1913, p. 12.

185   **"It then turned inward till it was flying on its back"**: Pégoud's loop is described in "Flies Upside Down for Quarter of a Mile," *New York Times*, September 2, 1913, p. 5.

Chapter 28: The Master Birdman Returns

190   **"aviation has changed from a dangerous pursuit to a serious business"**: Beachey's remarks were syndicated, for example, from the *Frederick Maryland News*, September 30, 1913, p. 6.

192   **"turned the aeroplane around twice on its own axis"**: Beachey's loop was widely reported, here from the *New York Times*, November 19, 1913, p. 1.

Chapter 29: Around the World

194   **"turned seven somersaults in a biplane"**: "Turns Seven Somersaults in Air," *Evening Star* (Washington, DC), January 5, 1914, p. 3, http://chroniclingamerica.loc.gov/lccn/sn83045462/1914-01-05/ed-1/seq-3.

195   **"expected to enter the race"**: Beachey's agreeing to join the around-the-world race from the *New York Times*, February 6, 1914, p. 2.

195   **"I am really sorry about schemes flaunted before the public"**: Beachey's going back on his agreement, quoted in C. R. Roseberry, *Glenn Curtiss: Pioneer of Flight* (Garden City, NY: Doubleday, 1972), p. 371.

196   **"promising to give a series of thrilling exhibitions"**: "Beachey Has New Stock of Thrills," *New-York Tribune*, April 18, 1914, p. 5, http://chroniclingamerica.loc.gov/lccn/sn83030214/1914-04-18/ed-1/seq-5.

Chapter 30: Looping Across America

197–88   **"He flew down the center, having to keep a straight course"**: Reports of Beachey's indoor flight were syndicated, with an accompanying photograph, appearing, for example, in *Ashland Tidings*, June 25, 1914, p. 6.

199   **"cleverest exhibition flying New Yorkers have ever seen"**: Description of Beachey's flights at Brighton Beach from the *New York Tribune*, May 23, 1914, p. 20.

200–201   **"Rain or shine, wind or calm, Lincoln Beachey"**: Richmond, Kentucky, *Climax*, August 5, 1914, p. 7.

Chapter 31: Flying for the President

202–6   **"I will do all in my power to…demonstrate…the advance…in aero-science"**: Beachey's exploits, his offer of service, and his sentiments about the future of aviation were described in every Washington, DC, newspaper. See especially, "Beachey's Daring Thrills Capital," *Washington Times*, September 28, 1914, pp. 1, 4.

Chapter 32: Monoplane

207   **"caused the doors of the exhibit palaces to open"**: "Exposition Opened at San Francisco," *Evening Star* (Washington, DC), February 20, 1915, p. 1, http://chroniclingamerica.loc.gov/lccn/sn83045462/1915-02-20/ed-1/seq-1.

208   **"two entirely new and death defying stunts"**: "Wonderful Exhibits from All Lands Show the World's Best Progress," *Perrysburg* (Ohio) *Journal*, March 11, 1915, p. 6, http://chroniclingamerica.loc.gov/lccn/sn87076843/1915-03-11/ed-1/seq-6.

209   **"My brother wanted speed"**: "Reminiscences of Hillery Beachey: Oral History, 1960," Columbia Center for Oral History, Columbia University Libraries, New York, NY, https://clio.columbia.edu/catalog/4072378.

209–10   **"he shot straight up into the air, climbing to about 5,000 feet"**: Beachey's last flight described in *Aeronautics* 16, no. 3 (April 15, 1915), p. 42.

211   **"like the breaking of a ship's mast"**: Hillery Beachey, "Reminiscences of Hillery Beachey."

211   **"Thousands of spectators rushed to the nearby waterfront"**: Beachey's crash described in the *New York Times*, March 15, 1915, p. 1.

SELECTED BIBLIOGRAPHY

Books and Articles

Anderson, John D. *A History of Aerodynamics and Its Impact on Flying Machines.* New York: Cambridge University Press, 1999.

Crouch, Tom D. *The Bishop's Boys: A Life of Wilbur and Orville Wright.* New York: W. W. Norton & Company, 1989.

———. *A Dream of Wings: Americans and the Airplane, 1875–1905.* New York: W. W. Norton & Company, 1981.

Curtiss, Glenn Hammond, and Augustus Post. *The Curtiss Aviation Book.* New York: Frederick A. Stokes Company, 1912.

Grahame-White, Claude. *The Aeroplane: Past, Present, and Future.* New York: Harry Harper, 1911.

Griffith, Linda Arvidson. *When the Movies Were Young.* New York: Benjamin Blom, 1925.

Hatch, Alden. *Glenn Curtiss: Pioneer of Aviation.* Guilford, CT: The Lyons Press, 1942, 2007.

Hedin, Robert. *The Zeppelin Reader: Stories, Poems, and Songs from the Age of Airships.* Iowa City: University of Iowa Press, 1998.

Herlihy, David V. *Bicycle: The History.* New Haven, CT: Yale University Press, 2004.

Hoffman, Paul. *Wings of Madness: Alberto Santos-Dumont and the Invention of Flight.* New York: Hyperion, 2003.

Howard, Fred. *Wilbur and Orville: A Biography of the Wright Brothers.* New York: Knopf, 1987.

Kelly, Fred. *The Wright Brothers: A Biography.* Mineola, NY: Dover Publications, 1989.

Kurtz, Gary F. "'Navigating the Upper Strata' and the Quest for Dirigibility." *California History* 58, No. 4 (winter 1979/1980).

Lebow, Eileen F. *Before Amelia: Women Pilots in the Early Days of Aviation.* Washington, DC: Brassey's, 2002.

Ludlow, Israel. *Navigating the Air: A Scientific Statement of the Progress of Aëronautical Science Up to the Present Time.* New York: Aero Club of America, 1907.

Marrero, Frank. *Lincoln Beachey: The Man Who Owned the Sky.* San Francisco: Scottwall, 1997.

McFarland, Marvin W., ed. *The Papers of Wilbur and Orville Wright.* New York: McGraw-Hill, 1963.

Mortimer, Gavin. *Chasing Icarus: The Seventeen Days in 1910 That Forever Changed American Aviation.* New York: Walker & Company, 2010.

Pauley, Kenneth E., and Dominguez Rancho Adobe Museum. *The 1910 Los Angeles International Air Meet.* Mount Pleasant, SC: Arcadia Publishing, 2009.

Rich, Doris L. *The Magnificent Moisants: Champions of Early Flight.* Washington, DC: Smithsonian Institution Press, 1998.

Roseberry, C. R. *Glenn Curtiss: Pioneer of Flight.* Garden City, NY: Doubleday, 1972.

Schwartz, Rosalie. *Flying Down to Rio: Hollywood, Tourists, and Yankee Clippers.* College Station: Texas A&M University Press, 2004.

Scott, Phil. *Then and Now: How Airplanes Got This Way.* Batavia, OH: Sporty's Pilot Shop, 2012.

Shulman, Seth. *Unlocking the Sky: Glenn Hammond Curtiss and the Race to Invent the Airplane.* New York: HarperCollins Publishers, 2002.

Spenser, Jay. *The Airplane: How Ideas Gave Us Wings.* New York: Collins, 2008.

Tobin, James. *To Conquer the Air: The Wright Brothers and the Great Race for Flight.* New York: Simon & Schuster, 2004.

Wright, Wilbur, Orville Wright, and Fred C. Kelly, ed. *Miracle at Kitty Hawk: The Letters of Wilbur and Orville Wright.* New York: Da Capo Press, 2002.

Websites

The Alexander Graham Bell Family Papers. Manuscript Division, Library of Congress, Washington, DC; http://memory.loc.gov/ammem/bellhtml/bellhome.html.

Chronicling America. National Endowment for the Humanities and the Library of Congress, Washington, DC; http://chroniclingamerica.loc.gov.

The Wilbur and Orville Wright Papers. Manuscript Division, Library of Congress, Washington, DC; http://memory.loc.gov/ammem/wrighthtml/wrighthome.html.

Wright Brothers Aeroplane Company; http://www.wright-brothers.org.

Periodicals

Aero and Hydro: America's Aviation Weekly 1–5 (1909–1913). Chicago: E. Percy Noël.

Aeronautics 1–17 (1908–1915). New York: E. L. Jones, by the Aeronautics Press.

Aircraft 1–5 (1910–1915). New York: Lawson Publishing Company.

Everybody's Magazine 20 (January 1909). New York: North American Company.

Munsey's Magazine 45 (September 1911). New York: Frank A. Munsey Company.

National Geographic Magazine 16 (June 1903). Washington, DC: National Geographic Society.

National Magazine 28 (July 1908). Boston: Chappelle Publishing Company.

Popular Science 110 (April 1927). New York: Popular Science Publishing Company.

Other

The Aeronautical Annual: Devoted to the Encouragement of Experiment with Aerial Machines and to the Advancement of the Science Aerodynamics. Vols. 1–3. Boston: W. B. Clarke & Co., 1894–1896.

Beachey, Hillery. "Reminiscences of Hillery Beachey: Oral History, 1960." New York: Columbia Center for Oral History, Columbia University Libraries, https://clio.columbia.edu/catalog/4072378.

Coffyn, Frank T. "Reminiscences of Frank T. Coffyn: Oral History, 1960." New York: Columbia Center for Oral History, Columbia University Libraries, https://clio.columbia.edu/catalog/4074043.

Havens, Beckwith. "Reminiscences of Beckwith Havens: Oral History, 1960." New York: Columbia Center for Oral History, Columbia University Libraries, https://clio.columbia.edu/catalog/4075358.

INDEX

Page numbers in italics refer to images,
photographs, and illustrations in the text.